IN PRAISE
OF FAILURE

IN PRAISE OF FAILURE

THE VALUE OF OVERCOMING MISTAKES IN SPORTS AND IN LIFE

Mark H. Anshel

ROWMAN & LITTLEFIELD

Lanham • Boulder • New York • London

Published by Rowman & Littlefield
A wholly owned subsidary of
The Rowman & Littlefield Publishing Group, Inc.
4501 Forbes Boulevard, Suite 200, Lanham, Maryland 20706
www.rowman.com

Unit A, Whitacre Mews, 26-34 Stannary Street, London SE11 4AB

British Library Cataloguing in Publication Information Available

Library of Congress Cataloging-in-Publication Data

Names: Anshel, Mark H. (Mark Howard), author.
Title: In praise of failure : the value of overcoming mistakes in sports and in life / Mark
 H. Anshel.
Description: Lanham, Maryland : Rowman & Littlefield, 2016. | Includes
 bibliographical references and index.
Identifiers: LCCN 2015037827| ISBN 9781442251571 (cloth : alk. paper) | ISBN
 9781442251588 (ebook)
Subjects: LCSH: Sports–Psychological aspects. | Athletes–Psychology. | Failure
 (Psychology) | Life skills.
Classification: LCC GV706.4 .A568 2016 | DDC 796.01/9–dc23 LC record available
 at http://lccn.loc.gov/2015037827

Printed in the United States of America

This book is dedicated to the memory of my parents, Bernard and Rochelle Anshel, who provided me with the opportunities to learn, to overcome adversity, and to successfully meet life's daily challenges. They "allowed" me to fail without humiliation—in school, in sport, and at work—so that I could build on, learn from, and grow as a result of these failures. Success eventually came, not due to good luck, favorable conditions, or money, but through hard effort. I thank my parents for teaching me to learn and live by my most important values and beliefs about how to live and succeed. These values included integrity, family, health, faith, love, sensitivity, character, happiness, genuineness, commitment, kindness, respect for others, empathy, and honesty. I also acknowledge their patience in providing me with the opportunities to experience a high quality education and to develop the necessary skills to write and teach. But perhaps the most gratifying quality they gave me was the desire and drive to make a difference in the lives of others. And that is a legacy about which I will always be most proud.

CONTENTS

PREFACE

Not only is failure in all areas of human performance inevitable in an imperfect world, it is actually *essential* to succeeding and performing at the highest level. I have failed on numerous occasions and in different contexts throughout my life. These personal "failures" have led to a very successful career. Despite suffering from not meeting the expectations of others, poor school grades (with consequential parental reprimands to make matters worse), and not succeeding at the elite level in sports, I can now objectively reflect on the tremendous opportunities that failure provided.

There are two main objectives of this book. The *first objective* is to improve our understanding of the value of failure as part of the process of growing and achieving, particularly with respect to all areas of human performance, such as sport, exercise, the arts—acting, dancing, musical instruments—and work settings. What we label *failure* is not, in fact, failure at all. Instead, what is often called failure consists of not meeting goals or expectations, or not achieving perfection. These undesirable outcomes are a component of learning, improving, and eventually reaching our optimal performance. We are wrong by juxtaposing the term and concept of *losing* with *failure*. Losing is an outcome of competition, not a component of failure. Thus, we often misuse the word *failure*, especially in achievement settings.

The *second objective* of this book is that we—as individuals, groups, and cultures—need to understand and accept failure, that is, not meeting performance expectations, as an integral component of achieving success in all areas of life. There is no success without failure—both perceived failure (i.e., the performer's own view and interpretation) and actual failure (i.e., an objective measure of not achieving a favorable or desirable outcome). Humans learn from mistakes as part of the processes of growth and development. Humans are imperfect; errors are inevitable. So we must use errors to learn and improve our performance. Our mission is not to eliminate mistakes in life. Instead, we should embrace our mistakes as building blocks toward eventual achievement and success. We need to interpret our inevitable less-than-perfect performance outcomes as what separates humans from machines. Errors give us our humanity and fulfill our inherent need to achieve. The worst possible response to making mistakes is to react in a hostile manner because we expected perfection.

The concepts of failure and success need to be defined and applied to sport and exercise settings. So-called failure is far more desirable and positive than many sport leaders, parents, performers, coaches, and athletes typically acknowledge. The best, highest, and most successful athletes have one characteristic in common: they failed often, using their failure to learn, improve, and eventually achieve at the highest level. To our most accomplished performers in sport and other performance areas, such as the arts, failure was a gift.

INTRODUCTION

Defining *Failure* and *Success* in Sport

Anyone who has achieved anything great, anyone who has changed the world, has at some point made a choice to embrace failure instead of fighting it.

—Zoë B (2013), life coach and founder of SimpleLifeStrategies

The concept of failure is both foreign and unacceptable in many cultures. As one high school coach told my team, "Only losers fail, and we don't play this game to lose." Perhaps not surprisingly, therefore, the fear of failing remains one of the most paralyzing mind-sets (and dispositions) in competitive sport. Sports performers can become paralyzed with fear when asked to engage in challenging tasks that can lead to the perception of failure—not achieving the performer's goals. One outcome of fearing failure is a related concept called *choking*, in which a person has previously demonstrated high skill, but fails to exhibit similarly competent performance under high-pressure conditions.

For some athletes the thought of failure induces enormous fear and anxiety. Fear of what? Anxiety caused by what factors? Fear of disappointing others—coaches, teammates, spectators—and of not meeting personal goals; anxiety caused by worrying about not meeting performance expectations.

To the athlete who fears failure, it is better not to attempt a task or be in a situation that might not be successful. Their self-talk is, "If I don't try, I can't fail." These athletes fear striking out with runners on base. They fear any situation that induces worry (anxiety) and possible embarrassment. How do high-quality athletes overcome these types of situations? How do they overcome fear? Chapter 6 on coping with failure will address this issue. Sometimes the underachieving athletes do not perform at their previous best and do not grow and achieve to their potential. This book is written for them.

Failure is an inevitable outcome that everyone experiences, particularly athletes in competitive situations. It is not failure that determines eventual success; it is how we perceive and react to failure. Athletes are in the unique position of having their competence tested with each competitive event. Media scrutiny often exacerbates the emotional and psychological effect of experiencing failure. The polar opposite of failure—success—is desirable but less achievable in the short term. What is important to realize is that life consists of contrasts. There is no "right" unless there is a "left," there is no "up" unless there is a "down," no "good" unless there is "bad." Perhaps the central theme of this book is that we cannot experience success unless we have failed, no matter how failure is defined and perceived.

DEFINING SUCCESS AND FAILURE

Marcie was a college competitive swimmer for a small college in the Midwest. She was successful and had aspirations to try out for the U.S. Olympic swim team as a sprinter. Her coach put a damper on her aspirations when he informed her that he expected her to swim two full seconds faster if he was going to support her desire to be an Olympic swimmer. Two full seconds is very challenging to accomplish because sprint swimmers, as sprint runners know, are going all out and that all-out physical performance has inherent restrictions, such as the athlete's genetics, growth and development, and extensive devotion to training. After three weeks of training, Marcie quit her college swim team. She felt the coach was overreaching by setting an excessively difficult performance goal. Her motivation to meet the coach's goal diminished and her failure to meet her coach's demands was becoming more and more apparent each day. Quitting eased the pain of failure.

What, then, do we mean by *success* and *failure?* In order to understand the meaning of failure, we need to know the meaning of its opposite concept, success, and how success and failure differ, particularly within the context of competitive sport.

There are two types of definitions, formal and operational, in understanding success and failure related to competitive sport and other forms of physical performance. Both success and failure are perceptions. That is, they are formed, defined, and labeled based on the athlete's standards and personal interpretation. Whereas success is considered a reflection of desirable sport performance outcomes, failure is the perception that the athlete's performance results were not desirable.

Success in competitive sport is formally defined as *experiencing a favorable result* and *turning out as was hoped for.* Success, as it is related to sport, exercise, and other areas of performance, is defined in this book as *completing an experience that meets self-expectations or the expectations of others, or achieving a desirable procedure or outcome. Failure,* on the other hand, is formally defined as *falling short; a breakdown in operation; neglect.* Failure in this book, on the other hand, is defined as *experiencing a process or outcome that does not meet one's own or another person's expectations,* the result of lack of effort, poor skill, bad luck, or situational factors.

While success is obviously a preferable outcome, failure should not be feared and necessarily avoided. Instead, failure should be embraced and viewed as part of the process of growing, developing, improving, and succeeding. There are many examples of failure that lead to success among the world's highest achievers—people who succeeded after initially failing. It has been widely reported, for example, that Thomas Edison experienced over 1,000 failures while trying to invent the light bulb. Whereas others would have concluded that Edison "failed" over 1,000 times to invent the light bulb, Edison concluded that he discovered over 1,000 times how *not* to invent the light bulb. Hall of Fame U.S. professional basketball player Michael Jordan was cut from his varsity high school basketball team and was sent to the junior varsity team for his sophomore (second) year in Wilmington, North Carolina. As described later in this book, Jordan missed more than his share of shots in his professional career. Many more examples of our well-known achievers will be discussed throughout the book.

To understand the role of failure in achieving success it is important to acknowledge that success and failure are both *perceptions*; they exist in the eye of the beholder. Most of what we call failure is, in fact, a component of future success. *Failure* would be more easily appreciated if we used euphemisms to describe it, such as *challenge, improvement, lesson, error detection, error correction, setback, lack of success, downfall, washout, shortcoming, underdevelopment, future growth, misfire, slide, breakdown,* and *weakness.* Failure, then, is just a label that represents negative and undesirable outcomes. Failure, however, can and should lead to success—the primary theme of this book.

Elite performers repeat this mantra: "I am not a failure (as a person); I failed at doing something." In the face of adversity, rejection and failings, great achievers continue believing in themselves and refuse to consider themselves failures. Instead of viewing failure as a final outcome, they use failure to gain information and to improve their performance. As author and television interviewer Tavis Smiley (2011) says, in his book, *Fail Up*, "accept responsibility, make amends, and recover."

FAILURE AND RISK TAKING

The dictionary defines *risk* as a situation in which there is the chance of injury, damage, or loss. To achieve goals and succeed in meeting needs requires taking risks. It could be said that everything in life brings risk. Life satisfaction is supposed to be a daring adventure. The less we expose ourselves to risk, the greater the chance of failure because we will not grow, mature, develop our skills, and expand our physical, emotional, and mental capacity to stretch our limits and improve. Our life philosophy should be, "I would rather try something great and fail than try nothing great and succeed." Under most conditions, achieving our goals is worth the risk of failure.

Why are we so afraid of taking risks, knowing that we will not reach our ideal performance state without doing so? In *Failing Forward: Turning Mistakes into Stepping Stones for Success*, J. C. Maxwell lists the following factors that demotivate people from taking risks:

1. *Embarrassment*: Risk-taking might mean failing, and that can prove embarrassing. An outfielder dives for a hit ball and misses, an ice hockey player attempts a pass in his own zone that is intercepted by the opponent, a swimmer anticipates the starting gun but is premature when taking off—these are samples of taking risks that may prove embarrassing. It is important to remember that taking risks is part of the process of improvement and success. It's about being comfortable with taking small steps and not caring what others think or say in response to small stumbles.

2. *Rationalization*: Some athletes are chronic second-guessers. They say to themselves, "Should I dive for the ball or let it bounce?" "Should I anticipate my opponent doing 'this,' or is it more likely he or she will do 'that'?" "Should I purchase top-quality athletic equipment, or is used or less expensive equipment good enough?" Former newspaper columnist Sydney Harris wrote, "Regret for the things we did can be tempered by time; it is regret that the things we did *not* do that is inconsolable" (Cook, 1993, p. 219).

3. *Unrealistic expectations*: Success takes considerable time and energy. Nothing is accomplished quickly if the outcome has long-term implications. Hard physical training, especially in the off season, consists of hours of hard muscular and cardiovascular work, and yet, there is no forthcoming athletic contest in which this hard training regimen will prove useful. Too many of our child athletes quit sport when skilled performance does not come naturally to them. Their potential to be a successful athlete is never tested. What a shame.

4. *Fairness*: Too many people consider themselves victims of their failed attempts at achieving desirable sports goals and fantasies. They are ready to offer a host of excuses for this outcome. Or they were treated unfairly by their coach—former or current—which explains the reasons for not performing at a higher level or not being given the chance to excel. Athletes need to keep a positive, optimistic attitude toward controlling their destiny and to overcome the excuse of unfairness.

5. *Timing*: Time is relative; if we waited for "the right time" throughout our life nothing would get done and our dreams and aspirations to excel would evaporate. Is there a perfect time to perform a task (e.g.,

physical training or practice)? Too many of us procrastinate by wasting time before we tackle a challenging task (e.g., writing this book). We need to schedule certain rituals that result in starting and completing tasks until the task is complete.

6. *Inspiration*: Some athletes want to wait for inspiration before they are willing to step out and take a risk. Some high achievers contend we must act on our insights and inspirations within 24 hours or it is likely we will never act on them. Most elite athletes had models and mentors who inspired them to greatness. When inspired, especially by others who have succeeded, we are more willing to take risks.

Most successful athletes believe that the secret to losing is to look beyond the failure; it's about how athletes perceive and react to failure that makes them high-quality competitors. They have to possess the ability to look beyond failure and keep achieving. Attempts to achieve require taking risks and remembering the strategies—thoughts, emotions, and actions—they used to become successful. Were the risks successful? Was the attempt to steal second base worth it? Did you "go for it" on third down and a yard to go for a first down? Did your strategy work? What can you learn from the outcome—successful or not?

A common phrase used when it comes to risking failure is, "What is the worst that can happen?" What is the worst-case scenario when risking failure? Will I pay a hefty fine, lose my job, be demoted (to nonstarting status in sport), be cut from the team, cause my team to lose, lose my friends and family, or receive a bad review by the media or from teammates? Or will I have learned from the experience and use this opportunity to get better?

How can the worst-case-scenario strategy be applied to improving sport performance in new situations? Failed experiences make us better. Athletes need to ask themselves, "How can I use the information obtained from this experience—performance feedback—and expand my capacity to reach my ideal performance state?" This book is focused on providing the strategies for achieving at the highest level, and understanding the reasons we need to praise failure. Check out the list of people who first failed before becoming famous.

Successful Business People Who First Failed

Achieving success is hard work. Numerous obstacles have been experienced by some of the best-known high-level performers. Failure, for these individuals, was met with harder work, effort, and determination. Here are some famous people who used failure as just the first step toward success (from "50 Famously Successful People Who Failed at First," n.d.):

1. *Henry Ford*: Car manufacturer Henry Ford was not an instant success. Early businesses failures resulted in having no financial resources five times before he founded the successful Ford Motor Company.
2. *R. H. Macy*: The owner of Macy's Department Store, now a national chain, failed seven times before achieving success with his store in New York City.
3. *F. W. Woolworth*: Before starting his own business, young Woolworth worked at a dry goods store. His boss told him he was not allowed to wait on customers because he lacked the necessary sense and skill.
4. *Soichiro Honda*: The billion-dollar Honda automotive business began with a series of failures. Honda's application to work for Toyota Motor Corporation as an engineer was turned down, leaving him jobless. He started making scooters at home and finally started his own business.
5. *Bill Gates*: Bill Gates dropped out of Harvard University and failed his first business venture with Microsoft cofounder Paul Allen. Gates eventually created Microsoft.
6. *Harland David Sanders*: Known as Colonel Sanders of Kentucky Fried Chicken, Sanders's secret chicken recipe was rejected 1,009 times before a restaurant accepted it.
7. *Walt Disney*: Walt Disney was fired by a newspaper editor because "he lacked imagination and had no good ideas." After that, Disney started a number of businesses that didn't last too long and ended with bankruptcy and failure. He eventually founded Disneyland and, later, Disney World.

1

HOW WE PROMOTE SPORT PERFORMANCE FAILURE

*Champions aren't made in the gyms. Champions are made from
something they have deep inside them—a desire, a dream, a vision.*

—Muhammad Ali (Lesyk, 2004, p. 37)

A common feeling among successful athletes, coaches, and leaders, in general, is that it is not rejection or failure that holds us back in reaching our performance potential. Instead, it is the way we choose to respond to failure that is the main factor that separates successful from unsuccessful outcomes after failure. Ultimately, it is what we choose to do—and think—in challenging situations that allows us to realize our potential and capacity to succeed.

According to publisher and commentator Arianna Huffington, "Failure is not the opposite of success; it's a stepping-stone *to* success" (Nelson, 2015). For most successful coaches and athletes, failure strengthens resolve and helps to cultivate a deeply held conviction about one's values and sense of purpose. Failure helps us focus on our mission—where we are going and how we are going to get there. In some ways, failure is actually *desirable* as a performance goal because experiencing failure is an integral part of finding success. High-quality coaches and athletes realize that failure is a means to improve and to reach and maintain optimal performance.

It is questionable whether it's in the athlete's best interests to actually promote failure. Some sports competitors possess certain psychological characteristics that have the unintended effect of encouraging failed performance; that is, their counterproductive thoughts and emotions lead to performance failure. While it is not true that some athletes actually *want* to fail, there are athletes who unintentionally set themselves up for failure. This chapter describes those psychological characteristics that have unintended consequences.

What does it mean to *promote failure*? In this context, promoting failure means that athletes engage in persistent thoughts and actions that inhibit sport performance, especially under high-pressure conditions. The interaction of personal and situational characteristics that influence performance is evident in an area of sport psychology called social psychology of sport. Social psychology of sport helps us understand how performance failure is more likely if an athlete maintains certain thoughts and actions, including *self-handicapping, social loafing, fear of failure, fear of success*, and *expectations for success*. Later we will examine additional features of the athlete's thoughts and emotions that lead to performance failure.

SELF-HANDICAPPING

First defined in nonsport settings by E. E. Jones and Berglas in 1978, self-handicapping consists of a person's thoughts and/or actions that serve to protect his or her self-esteem by providing excuses for failure. A sport example would be the athlete's anticipation of losing the sports contest before events occur by explaining reasons for the anticipated lack of success (Anshel, 2012). Self-handicappers externalize or "excuse" failure and internalize (i.e., accept credit for) success. They do not associate failure with their poor skills, thereby protecting their self-esteem. Thus, if athletes feel that they will not be at fault for failing—the expected failure is someone else's fault—they will not accept responsibility for group failure. In addition, the team, or group, is actually *expected* to fail. In fact, the athlete may unintentionally promote failure by exerting low effort. Thus, when we anticipate failure, we think and act in a manner that supports anticipated failure outcomes.

Here is an example of self-handicapping in a playoff football game between two teams with successful NFL seasons. The 1984 Chicago Bears football team knew that they were about to compete against the Dallas Cowboys, who had a superior record, at Cowboys Stadium—a home field advantage. As the Cowboys entered the stadium for the game, the home team crowd erupted in a deafening thunder of support. According to media reports, the combination of the opponent's talent and the stadium filled with screaming home team fans caused the visiting team to feel intimidated. Perhaps not surprisingly, the Bears lost the game by three touchdowns, partly due to negative emotions that caused them to feel distracted, worried, and anxious. "The stadium noise was a distraction," one losing team member reported.

SOCIAL LOAFING

If you have ever been part of a rowing crew, especially under competitive conditions, or if you have played tug-of-war, where opposing teams hold opposite ends of a long rope and individuals pull against each other, in unison and simultaneously, until one team is pulled across the middle dividing line, then you have seen social loafing in action. In tug-of-war, loafing occurs when single individuals on either side of the rope reduce their level of exertion and effort due to the assumption that their reduced effort will be compensated by others who are performing the same task simultaneously (Karau & Williams, 1993). The same thing can happen to a group of rowers or football players performing the same sport skill at the same time. Social loafing facilitates performance failure.

Other ways we set ourselves up for failure prior to sport performance include having high, often unrealistic expectations; extreme (neurotic, or negative) perfectionism; chronic anxiety; and irrational thinking ("I don't deserve to be successful"). More desirable thinking patterns that promote recovery from errors in sport include learned resourcefulness, self-control, confidence, optimism, facilitative anxiety, and making accurate explanations of performance outcomes, each of which will be discussed later. As writer and journalist George F. Will (1990) concludes from his extensive interviews of baseball athletes and managers, "The difference between the major and minor leagues is just a matter of 'inches and consistency'" (p. 270). Successful athletes do not loaf.

FEAR OF FAILURE

Fear of failure (FOF), also referred to as the motive to avoid failure, is a disposition to avoid failure and/or a capacity for experiencing shame or humiliation as a consequence of failure (Gardner & Moore, 2006). FOF is a fundamental belief of failure and associated beliefs that attaining desired goals is not likely or possible. Failure is often associated with predictions of social and familial rejection, expectations of external punishment, and a sense of reduced social value. Individuals suffering from FOF feel that attaining desired goals is not likely. Athletes with FOF tend to avoid training and preparation, which helps ensure their failure and reinforces their belief of future failure. FOF is a form of performance anxiety. FOF is related to low levels of optimism and high levels of worry, somatic anxiety, sport anxiety, and cognitive disruption (interfering thoughts).

FOF has a paralyzing effect on consistent and successful sport performance (Conroy, 2001). It expresses the contrary view that failure is good. Instead, FOF conceptualizes failure as something that is unhealthy, unhelpful toward future success, and something to be feared. FOF needs to be professionally treated by a mental health professional before people, including athletes, use failure for growth and eventual success.

FEAR OF SUCCESS

Do athletes whose prime objective in sport is to be successful actually fear achieving that success? Perhaps. The opposite of FOF is a psychological characteristic (not a personality trait) called fear of success (FOS), also called the motive to avoid success. FOS originates in one of five sources or antecedents (Ogilvie, 1968).

Some athletes fear the social and emotional isolation that accompanies success. An athlete may feel that isolation when performing at a level far superior to that of teammates. Athletes feel guilt by asserting themselves in competition. Certain athletes may feel uncomfortable exhibiting aggressive behavior, while others are not very competitive and would likely score low on any measure of competitiveness.

Another particularly fascinating source of FOS is the fear of discovering one's true potential. Such athletes' fears about succeeding are derived from fearing failure: FOS and FOF are two sides of the same coin. Perhaps athletes with a high degree of FOS or FOF should work with a sport psychologist to overcome, or at least minimize, these feelings. Withdrawing from further competition and playing sports under less threatening conditions (e.g., recreational leagues) remains an option.

Another source of FOS is anxiety—worry or threat—about surpassing a previous record established by an admired performer (Cratty, 1983). It is unlikely that most record holders in the Olympic Games or on professional

In July 1982 I attended a clinic on baseball batting given by the late Mr. Charlie Lau, then the hitting coach of the Chicago White Sox baseball team; the topic of the clinic was "what it takes" to be a successful major league baseball batter (Anshel, 1986). Coach Lau graciously agreed to meet with me at his South Side Chicago home for about ninety minutes about the psychology of baseball, with particular insights about batters. Coach Lau described many professional baseball players who were very gifted with the natural talent to become successful at the major league level. While many of these athletes demonstrated competence in triple-A baseball, he said, they were unable to demonstrate a similar level of competence at the major league level. He speculated that a primary reason for succeeding in the minor leagues but failing to match that level of competence at the major league level centered on the athletes' *fear of success*. In other words, some baseball players feared establishing standards that could not be surpassed in the following year, or that the major league level of competition was accompanied by the scrutiny, criticism, and analyses by the media, critical feedback (e.g., booing, unpleasant remarks) by spectators and opponents, and playing through pain and injury. Success, including competing at the highest level, has a price, including the ability to handle the pressure to succeed. Some athletes have chosen to remain within their comfort zone and not pay that price. One area that increases the chance of success at the highest level of competition is the athletes' expectations for success.

sports teams would be concerned that the previous record holder might be offended. Some athletes, however, might be intimidated by breaking a record previously held by a highly respected or admired athlete. They may also feel that others (e.g., fans, teammates, coaches, media) also resent the broken record.

A more common and likely source of FOS is preferring not to deal with the pressure to constantly match or exceed a previous best performance. According to Ogilvie (1968), trying to live up to the expectations of fans and the media can place an extensive amount of pressure on athletes to reach or exceed their previous best performance. Failing to achieve this standard may be perceived as disappointing and result in performance failure. This outcome is more likely to occur with some highly skilled athletes who lack competitiveness due to their discomfort with success. For instance, some athletes feel uncomfortable with the pressure of competing at an elite level and prefer a less-threatening environment. This disposition might explain why some athletes excel in minor league baseball, but do not do nearly as well at the major league level.

EXPECTATIONS FOR SUCCESS

One reason for upsets in sport—in which the team predicted to win and supposedly superior to their opponent surprisingly loses the contest—is that the superior team may not have perceived their opponents as threatening to their continued success (Ogilvie, 1968). Their expectation of success is too high, and the amount of effort they give is too low. Success expectations and athletes' motivation to achieve are influenced by the perceived ability of their opponents. In many cases, low expectations of success become self-fulfilling prophecies. In the opposite direction, however, high-quality competitors have a very high expectation of success: they expect to win—and they often do. Competitors are optimally motivated when they feel that they have about a 50% chance of success (Atkinson, 1957). In high-risk sports such as high jumping or pole vaulting, which require explosive muscular effort, expectations of success must be maintained or winning is far from assured.

Why do high self-expectations more likely lead to success than low self-expectations? There are several possible explanations:

1. *Greater effort*: It is likely that when an athlete anticipates success through high self-expectations, he or she will use greater effort and energy. Athletes are optimistic that their efforts will result in success, or that failure will be a better learning experience due to giving optimal effort.

2. *Attentional focus*: University of Tennessee motor behavior researcher Dr. Craig Wrisberg (2001) uses information processing theory to explain the superior mental processes of highly skilled athletes that lead to high performance quality and how processing information differs between highly skilled and less-skilled athletes. For instance, based on specific situational conditions, athletes need to determine if their concentration and attention should be focused internally (i.e., thoughts, emotions, feelings) or externally (i.e., scanning current environmental conditions). There are times when thinking should be at a minimum or inactive completely when executing a sport skill; the athlete performs the skill "automatically" with relatively little thinking. Other times, however, if conditions allow, the athlete needs to engage in preperformance planning and determine a preperformance strategy. Highly skilled athletes typically process information more quickly and accurately than their less skilled counterparts. Athletes with high expectations for success experience less mental interference and are better able to focus their attention on the most important features of the task.

3. *Information processing speed*: Sport events are often performed at a high rate of speed. Wrisberg contends that after stimuli (visual, auditory, tactual) are taken in by sense receptors, much of it is acted upon for immediate processing to determine what is important vs. what must be ignored and what warrants a rapid decision vs. what can be slowed down for making more accurate decisions. The athlete's reactions are based on a series of thoughts and decisions. Athletes with high self-expectations have greater capacity and less interfering cognitive (thinking) activity, which speeds up the rate of processing information.

4. *Superior anticipation*: Positive expectancies result in a superior level of anticipating the next stimulus (Wrisberg, 2001). This allows athletes to react more quickly to environmental stimuli and more quickly predict the location of opponents and the object in play than athletes who do not demonstrate similar anticipation skills.

FAILURE TO SET PROPER GOALS

One source of reduced motivation in sport is the failure to set and/or meet performance goals. Ostensibly, goal setting helps focus the performer's effort and provides a means to monitor progress, both successful and unsuccessful. A goal is what someone wants to accomplish; it is the aim of a person's efforts or the intention to reach a certain level of proficiency. The failure to set goals properly will likely result in the performer's view that the goal was not met and, therefore, the athlete failed to meet his or her own (or a coach's or parent's) standards. He was a disappointment; she failed. If an athlete sets an improper goal, however, the perception of failure would be erroneous. This is how we set ourselves up for failure.

There are two important points to be made about properly setting performance (e.g., sport, exercise, rehabilitation) goals. First, people differ in how they see the importance and value of setting goals. There is a concept called *goal orientation*, which means that some people find goals more motivating and relevant to determining success than others. If I have a low goal orientation, I am not likely to set goals because I will view a goal as intrusive into my own expectations. Goals do not allow for changing conditions over time and improved performance due to experience. For some individuals, goals are a distraction and reduce feelings of intrinsic motivation; performers feel less enjoyment and satisfaction from the activity.

The second issue to remember about goals is that they can set up the person for failure. If no goal is set, then doing one's best and accepting the outcome for what it is will be acceptable. Improving one's current performance in comparison to previous performance is interpreted as desirable—the performer was successful. But what if the improved performance did not match a predetermined goal? Is the performer to conclude that his or her performance outcome was poor—a failure? The argument against goal setting is that for some performers, goals are burdensome, not motivating, and in fact, impede the performer's concentration and level of satisfaction. Goals instill expectations, which breeds anxiety (i.e., worry, threat) and disappointment. This is especially the case for persons who are engaging in the activity for its own pleasure; there is no need to set goals to feel a sense of achievement or accomplishment. Thus, we set ourselves up to fail by introducing goals into the situation. Nevertheless, there are principles of proper goal setting that have the potential to increase performer motivation.

Here are guidelines for setting goals in sport and other areas of performance in no particular order of importance (see Anshel's 2012 review of this literature).

1. *Goals should be high and challenging, but realistic.* Setting goals that reflect perfection or are so high they are unlikely to be achieved reduces performer motivation instead of increasing it. As a young professor I had the opportunity to serve as a Division 1 college football team sport psychology consultant. The university had recently hired the team's new head coach. He informed the media and his players that his team would go undefeated in his first season. That standard of perfection was destroyed and discredited after the first game, which the team promptly lost. Sadly, he lost his job after two seasons.

2. *Goals should be observable, called performance goals.* How would one know if a goal was met unless it can be determined from visual evidence?

3. *Set both short-term and long-term goals.* Sometimes a goal is more effective and motivational if the outcome can be detected in a single practice session or within a few days. Other goals take much longer to accomplish and might be detected after the season or in a couple of months. Setting both is a good idea because it gives the performer a chance to build on early successes—meeting short-term goals—and making goal adjustments along the way if needed.

4. *Set process goals instead of (or in addition to) product/outcome goals.* The goal of winning is always nice, and so is receiving an award after the season (or at the team's postseason banquet). What is far more motivating and informative—because it allows for performance feedback and making goal changes—is to set goals that are detectable during

the season and give the performer something to build on. Examples of proper process or performance goals are: "I will attend at least 90% of practices during the first month of this season," or "I will accurately make 80% of tennis serves in practice this week." A separate goal would be set for match outcomes.

5. *Goals should be jointly set between coach and athlete.* It is rare for a goal to be accurately set if only the athlete has generated the goal. Coaches may have insights that will further challenge the athlete's initial goal-setting attempt. At the same time, coaches cannot set over-challenging, unrealistic goals that athletes will find virtually impossible to reach. In the introduction of this book I mentioned a female swimmer named Marcie who quit her college swim team because her coach set a speed goal—improving sprint speed by two seconds—she could not possibly match, especially in the same year of competition. She gave up after two months of trying to meet that goal, which was unrealistically difficult and had no basis given her past performance.

6. *Make goals personal; do not post the athlete's goal(s) in the locker room or other public place.* No one needs to know another performer's goals. That information can lead to public humiliation and embarrassment. An athlete's goal(s) is/are between coach and athlete.

7. *Performance goals should be measurable.* One coach asked his tennis players to set goals regarding "improved attitude" about competing, while another coach asked athletes to set goals that reflected their values. While well intentioned, both requests were impossible to generate and measure.

8. *Goals should be meaningful to each performer.* Perhaps a goal of studying 2 hours a day or running 10 wind sprints per day lacks meaning to the athlete, who prefers to study for as long as he feels comfortable or run wind sprints only twice a week. Being required to perform a certain time, length of time, or number of repetitions may be counterproductive to overall motivation, game preparation, and skill development.

9. *Finally, consider team goals.* If the preceding guidelines are followed, it is possible that team competitors will want to share certain goals that are meaningful to all team members and that support the overall goal of helping the team win. Examples include number of hours in

the weight room, attending "voluntary" practice sessions in the early morning, and volunteering to visit the children's ward in area hospitals. Not giving up after falling behind in the contest might be another team goal. Giving 100% at all times seems like a reasonable goal.

Failure is not avoidable, especially in relation to performing complex motor skills at a rapid pace, sometimes multiple skills at the same time. "To be human is to err," said the philosopher George Bernard Shaw. Error—and failure—are normal and even *necessary* components of achieving at the highest level. Learning is typically defined as a permanent change in behavior. For learning to occur the performer must fail, at first; interpret failure as a component of the end result of achieving; and then learn from failure experiences and make appropriate adaptations in eventually performance success. Winners conclude that there are no mistakes, only lessons.

At the same time, the content of this chapter reviewed areas of human behavior in which one's disposition and the conditions for performing sport skills make failure untenable and must be avoided at all costs. Certain dispositions such as fear of failure and fear of success, specific situational conditions such as self-handicapping and social loafing, and thought processes such as high self-expectations and confidence can strongly influence how we perceive failure.

Take, for instance, the practice of many sports coaches who are teaching our kids to hate exercise by punishing them with required high-intensity exercises following mistakes. High school coaches are still requiring their athletes to run laps and perform push-ups, sit-ups, and other forms of physical activity as punishment for making an error or losing. In fact, during my 20 months of employment at Texas Tech University (1999–2000) in Lubbock, Texas, I witnessed coaches requiring their team to run laps after *winning* the game. According to the coach, his team could have played better; they were not perfect. According to NBA all-star and Hall of Fame member Michael Jordan, "I've missed more than 9,000 shots in my career; I've lost almost 300 games" (Zoë B, 2013). No one is perfect! To the contrary, great athletes are literally dependent on making mistakes and experiencing failure.

The use of exercise as a form of punishment follows the old adage that if you punish a person for committing errors and not meeting performance expectations, she will play better and make fewer mistakes. Given the complexity of sport skills and the fact that competitive conditions make success relatively difficult to achieve, the practice of using exercise as punishment is entirely inappropriate and ineffective. In 29 U.S. states it is also illegal.

This book is about how to create an environment that embraces rather than rejects failure as a vehicle for reaching one's ideal performance state in sport and other areas of physical activity. Failure is not an event; it's a mind-set—a perception. There is every reason to make the perception of fear something to celebrate rather than dread. Good leaders don't give in to failure; they rise above it and use failure as a vehicle for learning, improving, and succeeding.

In summary, often it is the individual athlete—or coach—who maintains a mind-set (i.e., attitude, emotion, or way of thinking) that promotes, or contributes to, failure. The ability to identify factors contributing to failure is only a segment of using failure for performance improvement. The other component is identifying these factors to prevent thoughts, emotions, and actions that may contribute to failure; in other words, *long-term failure prevention*.

2

DIMENSIONS
OF FAILURE

Physical, Mental, Emotional,
and Values-Based

If you think about it, failure is just feedback; it's simply showing you what's not working so you can find out what will work. It's necessary and can't be avoided.

—Zoë B (2013)

A central tenet of this book—and in sport and life—is that failure is desirable in order to achieve success. In addition, failure is a *perception*. Becoming more and more comfortable with the "advantages" of failing requires understanding the four different forms, or sources, of failure: *physical, mental, emotional,* and *values-based* (sometimes called *spiritual*). This chapter addresses these four sources of failure, and how each can be converted to perceptions of *success*. We begin by defining each source.

Physical failure represents a person's physical performance errors or their tendency to engage in self-destructive behaviors such as overeating, lack of physical activity, intense chronic stress and anxiety, poor sleep habits, and rarely socializing or interacting with others. Outcomes of physical failure can lead to obesity, illness, disease, and even premature death. *Physical success*, on the other hand, can be achieved when a person engages in error-free or reduced-error performance, and maintains healthy habits related to exercise, proper nutrition and hydration, and high-quality rest (sleep)—all forms of recovery from life's storms.

Mental failure reflects poor (i.e., slow and/or inaccurate) thinking—called cognition by researchers and scholars—and information-processing skills. The result may be lack of, or poor, judgment and decision making, low retention of information, and the inability to separate important from unimportant information, resulting in information overload. Mental failure results in being easily distracted, quickly losing concentration, having poor anticipation skills (a particularly important feature of competitive sport), and having slow or limited storage of information into temporary (short-term) and permanent (long-term) memory. *Mental success* occurs when a person is fully engaged in a given task, can anticipate one's own or an opponent's performance, learns quickly, accompanied by storing an extensive amount of input, and is able to concentrate and to focus attention on the proper information.

Emotional failure is a person's inability to maintain emotional control, especially under conditions of stress, sudden change, and adversity. The person may be in a position of emotional instability, have highs and lows, and even exhibit actions that reflect mental illness, such as bipolar disorder, chronic anxiety, or depression. Arousal level must also be regulated, so that athletes who are over- or underaroused are not prepared to meet situational demands. Athletes must be able to regulate their emotions before and during the contest based on environmental conditions and situational demands.

Perhaps the best example of emotional failure is the well-known concept in sport called *choking*. Choking reflects an athlete's performance failure under pressure, as compared to her better performance level under low-pressure conditions. Choking, then, occurs when the athlete is unable to perform up to previously exhibited standards.

Emotional success reflects two things: the athlete's ability to (1) maintain emotional control, especially under challenging and uncertain conditions, and (2) create and maintain positive emotions that have energy-producing properties that are required to adjust to environmental demands. Emotional success occurs when the athlete maintains emotional control and applies the proper emotion at optimal intensity at the proper time or under desirable conditions in meeting performance goals for the task at hand.

A good example of choking occurred during the 2008 Major League Baseball championship series between the Chicago Cubs and the Los Angeles Dodgers. The Cubs won more games that season than any other National League team, whereas the Dodgers were the wild card team (winning the least number of games during the season among all postseason teams). The Cubs were surprisingly swept in three games, making five errors, one by each infielder, in the last of these games. Months later the Cubs manager, Lou Pinella, disclosed to the media that the players were "tight." Due to their superior season won-loss record, the Cubs were put under tremendous pressure to win the 2008 World Series. After all, the last time they won the series was in 1908, the longest "dry spell" of not winning the series among all major league teams. Not surprisingly, then, one additional source of pressure was that 2008 was the centennial anniversary since the Cubs last won a World Series.

The 2008 Cubs choked, and the team members, including the manager, knew it. A golden opportunity was missed to use mental skills to manage their stress and anxiety. Where is a sport psychologist when you need one?

Professional golfers have mastered emotional regulation. To break the tension, many golfers casually engage with their caddy or with others between shots, sometimes cracking jokes. The minute or two before taking the next shot, they focus intensely during a planned and ritualized "pre-shot routine" (Anshel, 2012). Baseball players take their practice swings during batting practice and during the game when they are next in line to hit, also called "on deck." But once they enter the batter's box they concentrate fully on the pitcher, and then engage in a series of pre-batting rituals prior to the next pitch. High-quality baseball batters filter out all extraneous noise, including the words of teammates and opponents, immediately prior to the pitch.

Values-based (spiritual) failure is evident when a person lives a life or maintains habits that are inconsistent with, or disconnected from, their deepest values and beliefs. Values-based failure also occurs when a person lacks passion about setting and making the effort to meet goals, and does not perform at his ideal performance level (see Chapter 11 for a full discussion of values in relation to exercise and other healthy habits, including a review of the Disconnected Values Model). Athletes are supposed to be models of good character, integrity, good health, and high performance quality. However, sometimes they falter by failing to demonstrate behaviors that are consistent with these values. Athletes, for instance, who test positive for banned performance-enhancing drugs are demonstrating values-based failure.

Values-based success concerns living life consistent with one's deepest values and maintaining a sense of purpose and passion during the journey to reach one's destination. Success reflects one's willingness to learn and perform with passion, and to make a difference in the lives of others. Success, in this instance, reflects one's satisfaction with the achievements of others and feeling partly responsible for their success. Elite athletes who are strong supporters of their family, who help teammates achieve at the next level, and who demonstrate behaviors that are consistent with their achievement status reflect values-based success.

Failure is part of the growth process and should be part of the celebration of personal and professional development. Failure expands our capacity physically, mentally, emotionally, and in accordance with our values. Values consist of core beliefs about what a person feels are important areas and priorities of life, that is, what they feel most strongly about.

PHYSICAL SUCCESS AND FAILURE

This component is more familiar to sports participants than any other because it is observable and represents quantitative performance outcomes; usually it can be measured more easily than the other components. In addition, the physical component forms the foundation of building and maintaining energy, good health, and high life satisfaction.

The goal for experiencing *physical success* is to address four areas of daily routines: dietary habits, hydration (adequate fluid intake), sleep, and exercise (and other forms of physical activity). Specialists are needed in each area to promote desirable habits for each of these areas. Proper dietary habits are needed to sustain high energy and good health. Meeting with a registered dietician (RD) is a good future investment because RDs have a nationally recognized credential that reflects the proper knowledge and expertise in dietary counseling; they know the science of nutrition and are capable of offering clients reliable and accurate information in meeting individual dietary needs. This includes developing ways to obtain adequate fluid—mostly water-based—intake that eliminates or reduces sugar and caffeine. Water is needed to cool down the internal body temperature and to eliminate toxins.

Proper sleep is needed to help the body recover from life's storms, build the immune system, and maintain proper energy. There are several guidelines for obtaining proper sleep. According to the National Sleep Foundation in Washington, DC, you will improve your sleep patterns if you (1) go to bed and wake up at consistent times during the week, (2) avoid stress and a large amount of food within 2–3 hours of bedtime, (3) do not place a television in the bedroom (because TV watching late at night tends to raise arousal level, which is stressful and keeps us awake), (4) avoid environmental sources of stress such as negative personal interactions and other forms of conflict at least 2 hours before bedtime, and (5) find out from someone who can watch you sleep if you snore and seem to be short of breath while sleeping; that is a sign of the sleep disorder sleep apnea, which must be addressed by a physician and formally diagnosed by a sleep clinic specialist.

Physical failure occurs when a person does not reach—notice I avoid the words *fails to reach*—preperformance goals due to any one of a variety of reasons. Like all forms of failure, physical failure is a perception. The athlete's behavior, or performance, can be labeled *failure* if the behavior is subjectively determined to be such. In this way, failure is in the eye of the beholder. Athletes have described to me the reasons they were not pleased with their game performance despite experiencing considerable success in the same contest. A football player might have missed a single tackle resulting in opponent success, yet he made several tackles that prevented the opponent from scoring. The athlete might conclude "I played badly" and yet the coach, teammates, media, and spectators might conclude the athlete played a high-quality game. Thus, physical failure should be based on preperformance criteria or expectations but, more important, should be used for the purpose of information feedback for learning and improving performance.

MENTAL SUCCESS AND FAILURE

Sport competition requires varying levels of concentration, attentional focusing, rapid processing of information, and the timely and proper use of mental skills. *Mental success* occurs when the athlete is fully engaged in a given task, can anticipate a stimulus or an opponent's performance response, engages in rapid learning, can make rapid decisions and react quickly to those decisions, and can select and process the most relevant stimuli in the environment.

Mental failure reflects the athlete's slow response to environmental stimuli, loss of concentration, mental fatigue, poor/inaccurate decisions, retention of relatively little information resulting in little or no learning, and inability to separate important from unimportant information. The ability to process information in short-term memory and to store and retrieve information from long-term (permanent) memory is impaired.

EMOTIONAL SUCCESS AND FAILURE

One area that separates elite athletes from their nonelite counterparts is the ability to control their emotions. Athletic competition brings out various levels of emotional intensity, also called arousal level, ranging from very low (e.g., golf, archery, dart throwing) to very high (e.g., football, soccer, boxing). Thus, it is essential that athletes be able to control their emotions.

Emotional success reflects this mental skill—the ability to maintain emotional control, especially under challenging and uncertain conditions. A related state of emotional success is to create and maintain positive emotions that alternately conserve and produce energy so that athletes can adjust their effort and arousal in response to changing situational demands. Emotional success occurs when a person maintains emotional control and can regulate optimal intensity at the proper time or under desirable conditions.

Emotional failure, on the other hand, is the athlete's inability to maintain emotional control, especially under uncertain conditions such as stress, sudden changes in energy demands, and demands of the task at hand. The athlete may be in a position of emotional turmoil and feel a lack of consistency—experiencing highs and lows, exhibiting inappropriate levels of aggression and anger, and perhaps exhibiting psychopathology (i.e., mental illness) such as bipolar disorder, chronic anxiety, or depression. Athletes must be able to regulate their emotions before and during the contest based on environmental conditions and situational demands.

VALUES-BASED (SPIRITUAL) SUCCESS AND FAILURE

Values are defined as a person's beliefs about what they consider important in life. To Rokeach (1973), values are core beliefs that guide behavior, provide impetus for motivating behavior, and provide standards against which we assess behavior. For example, an athlete who values commitment, responsibility, and health will tend to develop daily rituals and long-term habits that promote their high-quality sports performance and good health. Highly skilled athletes—and their coaches—feel passionate about their successful involvement in sport. Hours and hours of practice and physical conditioning are undertaken for the purpose of performing their best. Ideally, this passionate feeling is linked with the athlete's core values, that is, what the athlete feels strongly about and is integrated into their daily habits and lifestyle.

Values-based success is seen in athletes who live their life *consistent* with their deepest values. Their lives reflect their sense of purpose and passion about the level of expertise they want to acquire, what it will take to get to that level, and the development of an action plan that will help them reach their destination—in sport and in life. Values-based success also reflects the passion and commitment they bring to the sport venue and to make a difference in the lives of others. Success, in this instance, reflects one's satisfaction with the achievements of others and celebrating their success.

Values-based (spiritual) failure is evident when a person lives a life or maintains habits that are *inconsistent* with, or disconnected from, their deepest values and beliefs. Athletes who exhibit values-based failure do not set and meet goals, lack passion about their commitment to excellence, and claim to be willing to make sacrifices for setting and meeting high standards but fail to reach their ideal performance, partly due to a lack of energy and commitment.

The four dimensions of failure cover all aspects and characteristics of being a high-level sports competitor, reaching and even surpassing one's previous best, maintaining the energy needed to go to the next level of competition, celebrating the success of others, and being a good role model for younger, less-skilled competitors. Being able to handle and even embrace rejection is integrated into the equation of elite performance. According to television personality Tavis Smiley (2011), "Failing is part of the process.

No failure, no success" (p. 149). He says that "the key to success is self-knowledge and developing a vision of your life that inspires you" (p. 196).

Tavis Smiley suggests that we need to know what we can do; know our skills and not be persuaded to be someone we are not. "Know where your love is, and where you want to devote your energy to make a difference in the world," he says (p. 42). After we have established what we can accomplish, where we want to go, establishing our path in life, "we can start actually putting a vision together to get there" (p. 252). If your desires and values do not align with your destiny, start over and do what feels right. Just remember to be prepared to give 100% toward reaching your new destination.

California-based mental game coach Bill Cole (2008) suggests 10 ways to bounce back from defeat, making failure the start of a new venture toward success. He calls them Ten Powerful Turn-Failure-Into-Success Strategies. Here is an abbreviated version of these 10 points that capture the physical, mental, emotional, and values-based (spiritual) dimensions reviewed in this chapter. Winners, Cole says,

1. *realize that everyone makes mistakes.* The one way to prevent mistakes is to make no effort and take no risks. The best performers in all areas of life have achieved based on their mistakes; no one is exempt. The three certainties of life are death, taxes, and making mistakes.
2. *attempt to make fewer of them (mistakes).* The team making the fewest errors usually wins. The key strategy is error containment; take risks up to a point, but limit the errors that have potentially serious consequences.
3. *correct their errors.* People who commit mistakes but do not learn from them are making one more mistake. Move on from your mistake only after you have learned something from it.
4. *take responsibility for their errors.* Avoid blaming others for your mistakes. Get control over mistakes by admitting they exist and that you will not blame others.
5. *don't make the same mistake twice.* While perfection is impossible to achieve and, especially, to maintain, we want to put extra effort into avoiding a repeat of the mistake by maintaining alertness, anticipating the conditions and actions that may promote repeating the same mistake, and being on special alert to prevent it.

6. *fall fast and move on.* Failure allows us to verify wrong ways of doing things and to discard those practices that impede success. The best professional baseball pitchers claim that good hitters "own" the middle third of home plate, but that the pitchers must own and target the outer segments—about 4–5 inches on each side of the plate, what is called the "corners" in baseball nomenclature—to overcome the superb batting skills of high-quality hitters. If a batter hits an inaccurately pitched ball, move on but remember what happened.

7. *create a lifetime self-coaching system.* This system helps athletes see their errors, define them, accept responsibility for them, improve them, and maintain a positive attitude about the process. The best football athletes look at many hours of videotape and other forms of media *each week* in studying the tendencies of their opponent. Athletes and their coaches must collect data on their past performance to detect reasons why they are failing to match their previous best or what they must do to overcome flaws. They also want to know as much about each opponent as possible, particularly their tendencies and habits to respond in certain ways under particular conditions.

8. *view failure as just a detour.* Failure is not forever. Persistence is the key to being creative. Keep working on generating a positive outcome. Without becoming addicted to work, which is counterproductive, keep practicing, trying, and learning. Patience is a virtue. We need four things to get to the next level: a goal, practice, information feedback (often called knowledge of performance results), and motivation, which provides the necessary energy to learn and grow.

9. *know that failure is the teacher of success.* Failure is instructional. Learn a lesson every time you lose.

10. *admit that failure shows they are secure people.* We all have anxiety (feelings of worry or threat); in fact, anxiety is lifesaving when it's controlled and reserved for certain situations. Try crossing the street without looking out for vehicles, and one day you won't ever get to the other side. Let's not pretend we are impervious to choking—excessive anxiety that results in lower concentration and heightened muscular tension, both of which reduce performance quality. Show humility by asking people questions on issues you know little about, or who can provide insights into your weaknesses (e.g., a pitcher tips

off his pitches; a soccer or hockey goalie reveals her location to block the kick. Let's be secure with our limitations so we can get better and feel more confident.

Cole (2008) strongly urges us to build a master strategy of how we will react to mistakes when they happen. We need a plan for mentally handling errors and bouncing back from defeat—or the appearance of defeat. Finally, learn to apply these strategies soon, starting with those that come easiest. Collectively, they will take time to learn and apply effectively.

DIMENSIONS OF FAILURE ARE FUELED BY PURPOSE

If we know what drives our behavior, we will be comfortable with the inevitability of failure as a constructive process. As the need for our capacity to perform under adverse conditions expands, requiring more and more energy, various factors work to diminish or limit our capacity. Rituals, performed repeatedly and consciously until they become automatic, are needed to help to sustain our energy to reach and maintain optimal performance. We need to feel inspired and self-motivated to make changes in our lives in response to failure feedback. The status quo becomes unacceptable; we can do better. The process of acknowledging what is really important to maintaining good health, happiness, and life satisfaction, and of using our energy to have a vision about having a brighter future is called *purpose*.

Purpose consists of determining our most important values and living our lives consistent with those values. Then, we want to determine our vision of what and who we want to become, and develop a mission that will get us to that place. If we have a vision about what we want to do, let's say become a professional athlete or earn a college degree, then we need to develop a strategy to reach that goal (or set of goals). Purpose provides the fuel for the energy needed to perform the necessary tasks under the right conditions.

The second stage of reaching your vision, which forms your sense of purpose, is to state the truth about your behavior. Are you ready for the challenge of developing your strategy and moving toward reaching your vision? Do you keep in good physical condition to perform sport skills at the highest level? Do you seek information, coaching, and feedback from others who have insights into improving your performance quality? Is your nutrition contributing to your physical and mental preparation for performance success, or are you on borrowed time by consuming simple sugars and not eating strategically (i.e., consuming high-energy foods)?

The third stage is to take action that brings you closer to reaching your performance potential and living your life consistent with your values. The inconsistency between your values and any self-destructive daily habits or rituals is called a disconnect (Anshel, Brinthaupt, & Kang, 2010). The action phase consists of an action plan in which the performer carries out specific behaviors and strategies—mental and physical—that are consistent with the performer's values. Examples include snacks consisting of complex carbohydrates, such as fruit, instead of high simple sugar, such as candy; pre-sleep rituals to help ensure proper rest overnight; exercise that is conducted properly and during the week to improve various forms of fitness (e.g., cardiovascular, strength, flexibility/stretching, relaxation). The performer is fully engaged to meet self-expectations and task demands; effort to maintain one's ideal performance state is 100%.

Purpose, then, is about living one's life using rituals that are linked to one's values and beliefs about what's really important and needed to reach one's vision. Every elite athlete has generated the energy to expand his or her physical, mental, emotional, and values-based (spiritual) capacity to perform at the highest level, and particularly under pressure. Failure is used as fuel; it is experienced and perceived as an integral part of the process to learn, develop, grow, mature, and succeed.

Scientists and Thinkers Who Failed
Before Their Well-Known Success

The following examples come from "50 Famously Successful People Who Failed at First" (n.d.).

Albert Einstein: The name Albert Einstein is usually associated with brilliance and genius, but he had academic limitations in his early life. Einstein did not speak until he was 4 years old and did not read until he was 7 years of age. His teachers and parents concluded he was mentally slow and antisocial. He was expelled from school. Einstein went on to win the Nobel Prize and changed the face of modern physics.

Charles Darwin: As a young man Charles Darwin wanted a medical career. Sadly, he gave up on this wish, in part because he was often chastised by his father for being "lazy and too dreamy." Darwin himself wrote, "I was considered by all my masters and my father, a very ordinary boy, rather below the common standard of intellect." Clearly, this was a premature judgment. To his credit, Charles Darwin went on to become a well-known scientist.

Sir Isaac Newton: Newton was undoubtedly a genius when it came to math, but he had some early failures. He was not a good student and failed when asked to supervise the family farm. In fact, an uncle took over and sent him off to Cambridge University, where he finally blossomed into a scholar.

Socrates: Socrates was one of the world's greatest philosophers of his time—and beyond. However, not everyone appreciated his views. He was known as "an immoral corrupter of youth" and, consequently, sentenced to death. Socrates, however, did not succumb to these accusations. He continued to teach until he was forced to drink a poisonous substance, which killed him.

Dr. Robert Sternberg, psychology professor: This well-published psychology writer and researcher received a C in his first college introductory psychology class. His teacher informed him that "there was already a famous Sternberg in psychology and it was obvious there would not be another." Sternberg showed him, however, graduating summa cum laude and Phi Beta Kappa from Stanford with exceptional distinction in psychology, and eventually became the president of the American Psychological Association. This should inspire students at traditional and accredited online colleges to always strive to succeed, no matter what anyone says along the way.

3

EXPLAINING THE CAUSES OF PERFORMANCE FAILURE

If you look at the most inspirational innovators, athletes, ge-
niuses, and icons throughout history, they all shared a common
belief—they simply did not entertain the notion of failure as a
bad thing.

—Zoë B (2013)

All of us make excuses in an attempt to explain the causes of certain behavior outcomes. Here's a question: What is more motivating in response to making a performance error—telling yourself that you lack the skills to be a competent athlete or concluding that the error was on a very difficult play and that you have to keep practicing so that errors are less likely in the future? Along these lines, when high-quality baseball players strike out with the bases loaded, do they conclude that they lack the proper skills and, therefore, are not worthy of being a competitor at the elite level? Or might they conclude the pitcher was very good (or very lucky) on this occasion? What is the effect on the athlete's motivation if he concludes, "I'm not a very good athlete" versus concluding "I did not get a hit this time, but I know I can do better and will keep trying" after he experiences performance failure?

This chapter taps into the sport psychology literature concerning an area called *causal attributions*, or *attribution theory*. Attribution theory—explaining the causes of performance outcomes—is important because it has strong motivational properties. Making the "correct" (i.e., accurate) causal explanation following *perceived success* or *perceived failure* can strongly affect an athlete's desire to maintain participation, to expend the energy needed to improve, or to conclude that this sport or situation warrants quitting.

Applying attribution theory following perceived failure concerns explaining the causes of desirable (successful) or undesirable (unsuccessful) performance outcomes. The performer's motivation level is raised by making accurate causal explanations. First developed by psychology professor Dr. Bernard Weiner in 1974, the primary causal explanations following performance success and failure include high or low levels of *ability, effort, task difficulty/opponent*, and *luck* (see Table 3.1). We begin, however, with the two primary principles of using cause attributions for their intended purpose of motivating athletes: taking responsibility and making accurate explanations.

Table 3.1. **Attribution Model Based on the Four Explanations of Performance Outcomes**

		LOCUS OF CONTROL	
		INTERNAL	EXTERNAL
STABILITY	STABLE	Ability	Task Difficulty/Opponent
	UNSTABLE	Effort	Luck

TAKING RESPONSIBILITY

The opposite of taking responsibility for one's desirable and undesirable sport performance is *defensiveness*. The tendency to be defensive contributes strongly to stagnation, or the lack of personal and emotional growth, and the failure to perform better in sport and in other areas of life. Defensiveness consists of blaming others—or other factors and conditions—while not taking responsibility for undesirable outcomes. Of particular concern about defensiveness is that it reflects a person's inability to be objective in assessing the cause(s) of a problem or event, regardless of how obvious or even advantageous it might be to feel (and claim) responsibility. The purpose of defensiveness, psychologists tell us, is to protect our self-esteem.

High-level performers take responsibility for their actions, particularly when the cause of the performance outcome is accurate. In fact, sometimes elite level performers claim they caused—were responsible for—the outcome even when the evidence indicates they were not. A basketball player, for instance, may claim that she failed the team and might even feel responsible for the team's loss due to missing a free throw late in the game or making an inaccurate pass to a teammate late in the game, leading to a turnover and game loss. In fact, however, these athletes played an excellent game while making very few errors and scoring many points.

The essential part of taking responsibility and not being defensive in understanding our strengths and areas for future development in sport is (1) knowing which factor was primarily responsible for the performance outcome so they can respond accurately to the cause of their performance, and (2) establishing some degree of objectivity in confirming our perceptions about what factors caused our performance. Whose perceptions are accurate? What is the truth? Coaches should help athletes determine the factors that are responsible by offering information feedback on performance outcomes (e.g., "The error on that play, Marcie, was on a ball very difficult to handle; the batter made solid contact and it was a tough play").

Taking responsibility for the results of our sport performance allows us to separate mistakes from events that are unrelated to our skill level, to learn from our mistakes, and to put our new learning into practice in future opportunities. Learning from our mistakes requires acknowledging our role in experiencing favorable and unfavorable outcomes, and then moving forward with greater awareness of working on our weak areas so we improve in future opportunities. There is a saying: "It is easy to dodge our responsibilities but we cannot dodge the consequences of our responsibilities."

ACCURATE ATTRIBUTIONS

The second principle of explaining the causes of performance results is that athletes, and those who coach them, should do the best they can to explain the causes of outcomes as openly, objectively, and accurately as possible. As we will see in the following sections on the most common causal attributions, based on Dr. Bernard Weiner's (1974) model, different conditions warrant certain causal explanations. There are times, for instance, to explain success or failure based on (high or low) ability level, effort level, task difficulty (or the skills of opponents), and good or bad luck. Using the correct (i.e., most accurate) causal explanation for performance outcomes has strong motivational value.

I have counseled athletes for many years, and it seems the more skilled they are, the more likely they are to take responsibility for their performance. Well, according to the concept of "attributional bias," taking responsibility depends on whether they experienced performance success or performance failure (Anshel, 2012). High-quality athletes tend to feel responsible for successful performance (due to high skill or good effort), while failure is attributed to a superior opponent, difficult task, or bad luck.

For instance, the elite athlete made the basket in a basketball game based on his skills, but also took responsibility for making an inaccurate pass to his teammate that resulted in a turnover (i.e., the other team took possession of the ball). I had to point out the many times during the game in which he was highly successful and that sometimes the other guy is better—or just lucky.

HIGH AND LOW ABILITY ATTRIBUTIONS

Perhaps the leading reason people quit sports programs, including children, over 70% of whom drop out of youth sports under the age of 14 years, is because they explain failure due to perceptions of low ability. Therefore, undesirable outcomes such as losing the contest, making errors, or not performing up to expectations are due, they feel, to low ability. A low-ability attribution is a declaration of "I'm not good enough." That is, athletes who blame their own poor performance on poor skills, that is, explaining poor performance as being due to their low ability, are more likely to ask themselves, "Why stay in this unpleasant situation?" The "answer" to this question, too often, is quitting the sport due to a sense of helplessness (i.e., "I cannot control the bad current situation") and hopelessness (i.e., "Things are not going to change; it can only get worse").

We need to prevent these feelings from emerging among our athletes, but especially among younger athletes, who are more likely than their older counterparts to associate poor performance with low ability.

When we attribute *successful* sport performance to *high ability*, however, motivation becomes optimal. There is nothing that improves perceived competence—the fulfillment athletes obtain from achievement—more than interpreting a desirable outcome as being due to one's own high competence (i.e., high ability). The key issue here is to avoid attributing disappointing performance and undesirable outcomes to low ability as much as possible. Athletes and their coaches must also be accurate about attributing success to high ability. Sometimes it's best for athletes to quit sports in which their performance is poor or not improving, and they no longer enjoy the sport experience. Perhaps another sport or another position in the same sport are alternative strategies before quitting all forms of sport.

HIGH AND LOW EFFORT EXPLANATIONS

Expending effort in sport is highly controllable; you can exert effort at high, moderate, or low intensity—or not at all. It is the nature of effort, however, that makes this causal attribution so powerful and important. Athletes almost always attribute their performance success to high effort, partly because they train so hard and partly because it's true; high effort, fueled by heightened motivation and arousal level, often explains their performance success. High effort also reflects the athlete's training regimen.

On the other hand, attributing failure to low effort is "risky" because that may not be the true cause of failure. When a coach informs athletes they lost because they did not try hard enough, the athletes are being accused—perhaps unfairly—of being irresponsible and even selfish for not giving 100%. Athletes, on the other hand, may claim that lack of effort was *not* the reason they (or the team) failed. It was some other reason, such as the opponent's superior skills, a very difficult task (e.g., overcoming the opponent's strong lead late in the game), or bad luck (e.g., the game official got in the way of the play; the weather made the field slippery). Coaches who accuse athletes of not trying hard enough should provide some degree of objective proof or evidence of that assertion. "Low effort" is an accusation, and many athletes may resent it when they feel otherwise; that they were, in fact, giving 100% and the main reason for poor performance is that their opponent was simply superior. Remember, making causal attributions concerns motivating athletes, not insulting or humiliating them.

EXPLANATIONS OF HIGH AND LOW TASK DIFFICULTY/ OPPONENT'S SKILLS

The pitcher had a terrific fastball or curveball, the tennis opponent's serve was very fast and accurate, their soccer team was very quick and their goalie had great reflexes. All of these descriptions possess the common characteristic of attributing failure to an external source—superior skills by the losing player's opponent. This is a particularly important causal attribution because it is at the heart of sports competition: the other team or opponent was better.

No matter how much an athlete wants to be successful, there are people called *opponents* who want to win just as much and may have superior skills. The opponent's skills have to be taken into consideration when explaining performance outcomes because they inform the coach and athletes that ability level and effort were not factors in the outcome: "We lost the contest because the other team was better, at least on that occasion."

Attributing failure to a difficult task/opponent is particularly common among highly skilled athletes. Researchers generally agree that task difficulty attributions, similar to superior opponent explanations, are useful in maintaining the player's self-confidence, high self-esteem, and recognition of high ability. However, if the athlete's expectations of success toward the opponent are high, or if the high task difficulty or superior opponent explanations are frequent and ongoing, then explaining failure as due to low ability may occur. For example, "We continue to lose to this opponent because they are a good team, but also because our skills are inferior to their skills. We lack their speed."

Still, athletes must not approach the competition thinking they are at a disadvantage due to perceptions of opponent superiority, especially before the contest begins. That would perhaps result in *self-handicapping*, in which players set themselves up to lose due to their view that they are not good enough to win so why even try. They are already expecting to lose before the contest even begins. Nothing is more important than learning the requisite skills and performing them proficiently and consistently. Skill development improves performance and reduces feelings of helplessness for athletes of all ages, making "difficult task" or "superior opponent" less likely to explain failure.

GOOD VERSUS BAD LUCK

Just how motivating is it to explain the causes of performance success or failure due to luck (good or bad)? While performance outcomes sometimes do reside on luck—have you ever seen a slap shot in ice hockey go into the opponent's net after it was deflected by another player who happened to be positioned near the net?—attributing success to good luck has very little motivational value. How about a ground ball that goes through the fielder's legs for an error? Are complete contests won due to good luck or lost due to bad luck?

Attributing luck to a successful outcome may actually *decrease* motivation and confidence, while creating a sense of hopelessness about future contributions (e.g., "Can't I get credit for anything I do?"). Attributing failure to bad luck makes more sense if that is accurate (discussed in the next section) and is balanced by something positive that was accomplished; for example, "Our punt return man lost the ball in the sun and fumbled it away, but he also played an outstanding game."

ATTRIBUTIONAL BIAS

Sometimes explaining the causes of performance outcomes in sport is highly subjective and based on what "feels good" and provides the highest degree of motivation. Honesty and candor may not always help formulate the athletes' explanation. When athletes tend to attribute success to internal causes, that is, to high ability and good effort, and explain failure due to external causes, specifically, a difficult opponent or task or just bad luck, it is called *self-serving attributional bias*, or *hedonistic bias*.

Is this tendency necessarily a bad thing? Is motivation being compromised because an athlete feels better taking credit for success but not taking the blame for so-called failure? Probably not. Sometimes that's a good thing; attributing success to high ability or good effort builds self-esteem. However, there is a cost for not taking the blame for failure.

ATTRIBUTIONAL STYLE

Explaining the causes of performance outcomes is dispositional. That means athletes have a tendency, or disposition, to make certain types of explanations. Some athletes tend to take responsibility for their performance—good or bad—even if they should not, while others rarely feel responsible ("It's not my fault . . . "). These tendencies, often reflecting life's past experiences, personality, or the situation, are called *attributional styles*.

It is important to identify the individual's tendencies to make attributions that may or may not have motivational value. Inappropriate or inaccurate self-blame, for example (e.g., "It's my fault" or "I am really awful at that and I won't improve"), can reduce motivation and be very damaging to confidence and self-esteem, leading to feelings of hopelessness and, perhaps, sport dropout. Distorting causal attributions—for instance, externalizing the reasons for failures—prevents or inhibits the athlete's ability to use failure and disappointment as a source of incentive for future performance. Learning from mistakes is less likely. We can and should educate athletes and their coaches to make more accurate, constructive, and motivational causal attributions.

STOPPING THE BLAME GAME

The "blame game" consists of the style, or disposition, of not taking responsibility for failure or when the group's goals are unmet. The mantra for this condition is "It's not my fault" or "I just carried out orders." If the outcome is successful, then the person is more likely to claim credit, attributing high ability or high effort. If, however, the outcome was undesirable, perhaps falling below expectations and labeled a failure, then the blame game player is more likely to avoid taking responsibility. To play the blame game, failure and fault are inseparable; admitting failure means accepting responsibility. Perhaps too often we replace the word *responsibility* with *blame*, and use of the latter word has a more negative and threatening impression. If we stopped blaming and started acknowledging responsibility, perhaps we—culturally and individually—would more likely benefit from so-called failure.

Many leaders do not easily respond constructively to their perception of failure. Some people are motivated to work hard to overcome failure only if they receive blame for the disappointing outcome. Sports teams, however, can consist of a culture that makes it acceptable to admit and report failure, yet still foster high performance standards. That may depend on the failure's *cause*.

BLAMEWORTHY OUTCOMES

Some failure outcomes are blameworthy—finding fault with one or more individuals for the undesirable outcome—while some are not. *Deliberate deviance*—that is, purposely not doing the right thing or not trying hard (failing to make an optimal effort)—appear to warrant blame. Not being given the correct instructions, using a faulty strategy, engaging in improper or inadequate preparation for the contest, or experiencing failure due to mental or physical fatigue may not warrant blame.

There are two clear leadership strategies regarding blame. First, the criteria for taking responsibility for failure should be clearly discussed in advance of the season, contest, or some other period of time. For instance, an athlete who ingests a drug that is known to be banned by the league or organization, gets caught in a drug test, and is suspended for a period of time in accordance with the league's policy must accept full blame for the behavior and its consequences. Not following the rehabilitation program following an injury, resulting in a prolonged recovery period, is another example.

The second leadership strategy is that failure should not result in job termination unless the consequences of failure are dire—even potentially deadly—or the action that caused failure clearly indicated a lack of preparation or professionalism by the faulted individual. Competing aggressively in order to overcome an opponent's skills, a process called instrumental aggression, is within the contest rules. Being overly aggressive, however, perhaps resulting in an opponent's injury and resulting in a game penalty, game dismissal, suspension, or a more serious penalty of the offending player is not acceptable. This is clearly performance failure resulting in accepting blame and having consequences. These consequences, through which the team leader sets limits on inappropriate behavior, must be discussed before the season begins or employment with the organization is secured.

AVOIDING THE BLAME GAME

Mistakes fall into three broad categories: preventable, unavoidable (complexity-related), and intelligent.

Preventable failures. Most preventable failures cannot be harmless and ignored. Preventable failures might result from lack of proper training and support. Sports team members are encouraged to spot problems or even potential problems, such as an unstable part of the playing environment, lack of proper equipment, perspiration not being removed from the playing surface, or faulty equipment. This should result in a diagnostic and problem-solving process. Athletes might notify their coach that an opponent has a certain performance tendency in response to a particular game situation so a strategy can be planned that counters the opponent's tendency.

Unavoidable failures. Sometimes work tasks are complicated and errors are both common and likely. Perhaps problems associated with the sports team, opponent, or playing conditions create problems, even for the first time. While some errors can result in serious consequences, the mentality that all errors are bad is counterproductive. Errors, injuries, accidents, and performance limitations sometimes result from a series of relatively small failures that went unnoticed; for example, a player is out of position, the opponent attempts a new and unexpected play or strategy, a teammate makes an unexpected error, the weather makes the playing surface difficult to navigate, or it is a difficult play to make successfully. All are examples of small events in sport that can turn into game-changing outcomes. Failure happens.

Intelligent failures. Sometimes failures are *beneficial* and can lead to important insights into the problem or process. Planned "intelligent" errors can provide new valuable knowledge that can improve the team's future growth and development. Sometimes experimentation is necessary. Can this player provide the team with better performance if she bats lower in the batting order? Does a particular pitcher struggle when entering the game in high-pressure situations? Which team player can most likely make the final free-throw shot under pressure? Should we emphasize defense with five minutes to go in the game, and can our team adequately apply our defensive strategy? Should we attempt X play at this stage of the game with the current score? Failures mean that the outcome was not successful, but that experience provided invaluable information about future strategy and performance.

CAUSAL ATTRIBUTIONS AND THE KEY TO SUCCESS: ACCURACY

Performers—athletes, exercisers, musicians, actors, rehabilitation patients—can explain performance outcomes in any manner that makes them feel better and motivated. However, improved motivation and physical performance cannot be derived from "feel-good" attributions that are based on deception, defensiveness, or deceit. In other words, only causal explanations that are, or at least appear to be, accurate and true are likely to result in improved short-term and long-term motivation.

Coaches and athletes need to explain the causes of their performance in a manner that is *accurate*, informs athletes about their competence and achievement, and provides athletes with the level of motivation needed to remain on task. How can we deliver messages in explaining apparent failure that will prevent athletes from feeling discouraged, helpless about a brighter future, and even quitting sport? The skill to apply attribution theory goes a long way toward performing its most important function—to motivate the athlete and to keep him interested in maintaining and improving his level of performance over the season and beyond. As former British prime minister Winston Churchill said, "Success is going from failure to failure without loss of enthusiasm" (Cook, 1993, p. 515).

Perhaps the final word on explaining the causes of performance outcomes is that failure is inevitable—even necessary. Television interviewer Tavis Smiley (2011, p. xvi) describes it this way:

> If one dies at 39, like Martin [Luther King] and Malcolm [X], or if one lives to be 139 years old, you're not going to get it all done. There are going to be ideas you will never develop, projects you will never complete, conversations you will never have, people you will never meet, places you will never go, relationships you will never establish, forgiveness you will never receive, and books and speeches you will never write or deliver. We all die incomplete. . . . Failure is an inevitable part of the human journey. *Fail up* is the trampoline needed when you're down. When you take the time to learn your lessons, when you use those lessons as stepping-stones to climb even higher than you were before, you transcend failure—you "fail up."

4

FAILURE IMPROVES INTRINSIC MOTIVATION

The most inspirational innovators understood that every failure encountered brings you one step closer to success, and that this is a natural part of the process. Some even enjoyed failure.

—Zoë B (2013)

It's an oxymoron—an inconsistency—to claim that failure actually promotes motivation, considering that in most cultures failure is perhaps the ultimate de-motivator. Repeatedly viewing performance as a failure, or not meeting expectations, is more likely to reduce confidence, raise anxiety, and possibly result in quitting the team (dropping out). And, yet, highly skilled athletes persist and overcome adversity because they perceive their errors and other forms of undesirable performance as temporary, not permanent, setbacks.

MOTIVATIONAL VALUE OF PERCEIVED FAILURE

Perceived failure can serve as a strong motivator to improve performance and to feel a sense of accomplishment and achievement. Failure can be a source of inspiration and long-term commitment under the condition that the athlete maintains high expectations of future success and perceives early failures as an integral part of the building and learning process. This is the motivating property of failure; like life, we get better and overcome our shortcomings and limitations. Before addressing how failure can be a source of motivation, we need to define the types of motivation that most strongly influence athletes.

The important issue that builds motivation following perceived failure is that the perception of "failed" performance is accompanied by one or more "benefits." You learned to take a chance (risk); you learned more about your opponent's strengths or skills; you learned more about your limitations and what to work on, for example, building physical strength, improving your cardiovascular endurance, and enhancing your *mental* game (e.g., building confidence, feeling in better control of the situation or of rapidly changing conditions before or during the contest, improving the ability to anticipate your opponent's next moves, managing anxiety, improving the ability to cope with stress during the contest). Experiencing failure can improve motivation by turning a bad, unpleasant experience into a good, positive one.

DEFINING MOTIVATION

The term *motivation* is derived from the Latin word *movere* meaning "to move." Motivation provides the energy and direction to initiate and maintain behavior. Motivation has been formally defined as the tendency for the predetermined and planned behaviors to be controlled by their consequences and for behavior to persist until a goal is achieved (Alderman, 1974; Anshel, 2012). Let's review each segment of this rather formal definition in the context of competitive sport.

The *direction* of motivation refers to the purpose and the focus of the activity that will lead to a desirable outcome. The motivated athlete is energized to engage in a purposeful and meaningful task. Whether the task is physical training for sport or learning and practicing sport skills, motivated behavior is focused; it has purpose and a destination. Sometimes skilled athletes are required to change positions (e.g., a catcher is able to play first base; a football guard is switched to tackle). They should be highly motivated given the focus of their performance in achieving one or more specific goals. The athlete's motivation has to have a purpose—motivated to do what, exactly?

Deciding which task(s) to perform is *selectivity of behavior.* At times, a coach needs to inform athletes what he considers the most important skills or subskills to practice, learn, and achieve on a regular basis. At the same time, input from athletes is needed to determine if they feel comfortable learning new skills or changing positions as part of the skill-building process. Except to meet biological needs (e.g., hunger, thirst, sleep), motivation is rarely automatic and requires conscious thought and planning. There are different types of motivation. The types being reviewed in this chapter and that have the closest influence on failure are *intrinsic and extrinsic motivation* and *achievement motivation.*

INTRINSIC AND EXTRINSIC MOTIVATION

Intrinsic motivation (IM) is usually defined as "doing an activity for its own sake, for the satisfaction inherent in the activity" (Ryan & Deci, 2007, p. 2). Ryan and Deci contend that IM has a dual meaning. On one hand, IM concerns a person's innate tendency to act, rather than behavior being externally initiated and directed. It is natural, they contend, for athletes to respond to performance demands with optimal effort, anticipated success, and the avoidance of disappointment. On the other hand, IM refers to the fact that the rewards accrued from an activity are inherent in the activity itself—having the skill set needed to perform successfully and winning the contest—rather than being important to reducing biological drives (e.g., sleep, eating, drinking). Engaging in an activity, not just the outcomes from that activity, creates its own rewards.

For example, a person who finds the act of jogging to be pleasurable, and without reliance on the outcome from the jogging activity (e.g., weight control, improved fitness, winning a race), is intrinsically motivated to keep jogging. Failure will lead to personal growth and performance improvement more quickly and efficiently *if the person feels a sense of accomplishment and competence, and integrates positive and negative/critical information as part of performance feedback content.*

Persisting in an activity due to some external reason (e.g., money, recognition, prestige, an externally imposed requirement) and in the absence of pleasure and satisfaction reflects extrinsic motivation (EM). EM may explain why so many novice exercisers drop out of exercise programs; they are all motivated to exercise by outcomes (usually related to weight and body appearance) that take many weeks to achieve. The exercising itself is rarely pleasurable to the novice exerciser because we are a culture that does not promote physical activity; we literally "train" our body to be sedentary.

Deci's intrinsic motivation (IM) theory, formally called *cognitive evaluation theory* (Deci, 1975), also posits that every reward associated with IM has two components—a *controlling* aspect (called *self-determination*) and an *informational aspect* (positive or negative)—that provides the person with information feedback about his or her competence (i.e., the self-perception of one's level of skill and performance). The controlling (self-determination) aspect of IM represents the athlete's choice or decision to engage in the activity without being coerced or forced to perform the activity by another person. Thus, parents who dictate which sport or team position their athlete son or daughter will play are reducing their child's IM; self-determination is low. However, an athlete who is competing in a sport or playing a position of her own choosing is demonstrating high self-determination and, therefore, building IM. Taken together, failure *can* improve IM, which is the form of motivation that most likely results in a long-term commitment to performance improvement.

STRATEGIES FOR BUILDING IM

Intrinsic motivation is always more desirable than extrinsic motivation. There is no downside to participating in a contest, learning a skill, competing in sport, starting or maintaining an exercise program, or engaging in any desirable activity because of the enjoyment, satisfaction, or fun it brings the participant. Whereas EM remains a source of motivation, when that source is eliminated, let's say the trophy or going for a fast food treat after the team wins but going straight home after the team loses, motivation is either drastically reduced or eliminated. This is one argument against awarding trophies to recognize success in sport. When the trophies stop coming, so does the motivation to keep playing—or so it is thought. There is no downside to IM. Here are some ways to build and maintain IM in sport (see Anshel, 2012, for a more elaborate discussion of IM and IM strategies).

1. *Teach athletes to feel motivated to demonstrate competence, not only to win.* Building IM is more efficient if the athlete's motives to participate are based on what is called a mastery, or task, orientation rather than a win, or ego, orientation. The former (task, mastery) means that athletes are motivated based on their personal desire to achieve and demonstrate mastery of skills. The latter (ego, win), on the other hand, represents a source of motivation based on the desire to win, to beat an opponent. Coaches and parents should encourage the task/mastery orientation.

2. *Provide positive information early.* Coaches in sport, especially for younger age groups, can virtually guarantee success by providing positive feedback to athletes on some aspect of their performance. Athletes can be complimented for apparent improved skill mastery— if it is an accurate and honest performance appraisal—and for their effort in giving 100% toward experiencing a desirable performance outcome. Attributing success to effort or improvement is a virtual guarantee that athletes will interpret their performance in a positive manner, and that raises IM.

3. *Help athletes to learn new skills as soon as possible.* Coaches, physical education teachers, and, perhaps, the athletes' parents can provide opportunities for sport skill instruction and practice, thereby promoting early skill development. Ideally, fundamental skills should be mastered for that particular sport *before* they are required to be performed in competition.

4. *Help athletes select the sport in which they wish to engage.* IM is strengthened if the athlete has selected the sport (and, hopefully, the position within that sport) in which he or she chooses to participate. The athlete should play only those sports in which he or she feels most comfortable, finds pleasant, and is likely to succeed. In addition, younger athletes should be allowed to compete in more than one sport

or to change sports until (and if) they find one particular sport that they consider their primary sport.

5. *Use trophies and other awards based on a specific competency.* Awarding trophies to athletes "just for showing up"—called Participant Awards—has become very controversial in recent years (see Chapter 9 for a more elaborate discussion of this issue). Typically, these awards do not build IM; instead, they build EM in which athletes consider their sport involvement successful and fun if they "won" an award. However, one factor at the heart of IM is perceived competence. If the trophy (or some other award) is a reflection of the athlete's competence, the award should improve IM.

6. *Never attach recognition, approval, affection, and love to sport outcomes.* Conditional love is defined as showing affection, approval, or recognition to a child *only* if he or she has met some predetermined condition, such as successful sports performance or winning a contest. Unconditional love occurs when a parent (or adult) offers these same qualities—recognition, approval, affection, love—no matter what happens during the contest, win or lose. Unconditional love breeds all components of IM and increases the child's security and self-esteem. Sport enjoyment is far more likely than if the young athlete is unsure if he or she is accepted and secure with parental approval. Conditional love teaches the child that parental love is dependent on sport success; winning is more important than improvement and skill development. The source of motivation is extrinsic.

7. *Maintain a pleasant and enjoyable, not a negative and combative, competitive atmosphere in youth sports.* It is essential to remember that the ultimate goal of keeping athletes involved in sport is to ensure that the experience is enjoyable and fulfilling—even fun. So many children have dropped out of sport and are leading sedentary, unhealthy lives, often due to having negative experiences as youth sports participants. Younger athletes lack the skills, emotional maturity, and knowledge needed to perform at the highest level in sport. Adults have a crucial role in supporting this part of young athletes' lives, teaching them to worry less about the game's outcome and more about building skills, helping them stay active, and encouraging their desire to keep playing. Child athletes are not miniature adults.

GOAL ORIENTATION THEORY

Goal orientation theory (GOT) (Duda, 1992) reveals how failure can build IM. GOT is based on two sources: *ego*, also called win/competitive orientation, and *mastery*, also referred to as task orientation. *Ego orientation* represents the degree to which the athlete is motivated to engage in sport for the purpose of winning. Ego-oriented athletes are motivated by (1) comparing their skills with others, mostly opponents, but sometimes teammates, and (2) demonstrating superior competence. *Mastery orientation* consists of the athlete's motivation (1) based on performance effort and improvement and (2) to perform at one's best. Winning would be a natural outcome of improvement.

Athanasios Papaioannou and Olga Kouli (1999) contend IM is more likely to occur when the athlete is task involved, that is, when skill development and improved performance (following initial failure) are experienced. Ego-involved motivation, in which determining competence through winning is a priority, is less likely to induce IM. The association between task-involved motivation and IM is because task-involved athletes tend to engage in activities for pleasure or satisfaction. These athletes are focused on succeeding in the task at hand and attempting to accomplish short-term and long-term goals. Failure provides the impetus—the sense of challenge and self-motivation—to improve. Former CEO of Procter and Gamble, A. G. Lafley, has said he thinks of his failures as a gift for improving the quality of his leadership performance (Dillon, 2011).

Ego-involved athletes, on the other hand, view performance outcome—winning and losing rather than performance quality—as most important. The problem with dependency on performance outcome is that the end result is often not under the athlete's control. Opponents may have other ideas rather than to lose the contest.

All athletes want to win, of course. But winning affects the motivation level of task/mastery-oriented athletes differently than it affects ego/win-oriented athletes. Athletes who possess a high task (mastery) orientation are motivated primarily from demonstrating high competence. High ego/win-oriented athletes, on the other hand, are more motivated by performance and contest outcomes (i.e., winning or success). Ego-oriented athletes conclude that losing the contest reflects low competence and, therefore, are less motivated. Losing is commensurate with failure and therefore is not motivational. The ego-oriented athlete will not necessarily be motivated by meeting short-term performance goals unless meeting these goals is accompanied by a successful contest outcome—winning. Effort and performing one's best are associated with task/mastery goal orientation, whereas performance outcome (winning) is linked to ego (win) goal orientation. Thus, *experiencing failure is more likely to be motivational for task/mastery-oriented athletes than for win-oriented athletes.*

ACHIEVEMENT MOTIVATION

According to most personality studies, one characteristic of successful athletes—and individuals who succeed in other areas, too—is their high need to achieve. This need, which reflects a person's disposition (personality trait) and cannot be directly observed, is commonly referred to as *achievement motivation.* The central focus of this theory is that some individuals derive tremendous satisfaction from success in achievement activities. Each individual is responsible for determining his or her own achievement behavior, and defining success.

Success is based on the individual's perception that optimal effort will lead to achieving a desirable outcome and meet the athlete's goals. Individuals with a high need to achieve "tend to maintain a fervent and optimistic belief that success is possible" (Duda & Hall, 2001, p. 418). This is one reason high-need achievers prefer challenging rather than easy activities. Duda and Hall conclude that "immense satisfaction may be experienced when it can be seen that trying hard to overcome difficult challenges results in success" (p. 418). Thus, if the performance outcome is viewed as a result of the person's effort and skill, then the outcome is interpreted as successful, and this interpretation is highly motivational to athletes with a high need to achieve.

What is success for one athlete (e.g., getting two hits in four at bats in baseball) may be viewed as failure for another athlete, especially if performance failure occurred in crucial game situations that altered the contest's outcome. Of course, in reality, life is a bit more complicated. For example, when playing against a superior opponent some athletes do not even try because they predict that they do not have a chance to succeed. According to achievement motivation theory, these competitors will not necessarily interpret losing as failure because they didn't even try. "Blame" for losing is usually attributed to low effort, not due to the athlete's poor ability or lack of skills.

THERE IS NO SUCCESS WITHOUT FAILURE—
THE ULTIMATE MOTIVATOR

At the heart of this book is that "proper" views of situations that follow failure can serve as a strong motivator to improve performance and to feel a sense of accomplishment. Failure can be a source of inspiration and long-term commitment to desirable outcomes if the individual maintains high expectations of future success and perceives early failures as an integral part of the building and learning process. According to television host Tavis Smiley (2011), "Most people who have ever succeeded in any human endeavor will tell you they learned more from their failures than they ever learned from their successes" (p. ix).

MOTIVATION FROM HIGH ACHIEVERS
WHO ACKNOWLEDGE PAST FAILURE

We have so much to learn and use when people who are at the top share with others how they failed and how they handled it. Smiley (2011) claims that

> very few [high] achievers want to show off their warts by acknowledging the mistakes they've made along the way, much less put them in a book. I think that's unfortunate. Millions of people struggle with what it means to be successful, and the lesson they take away from successful folks who hide or deny their failures leads to an artificial construct of success. By "artificial" I mean the notion that people become successful without success scars. Let me be clear: There is no success without failure. Period. And usually a lot of it (p. x).

Sadly, many successful athletes refrain from admitting earlier failures. It masks their current achievement and their insecurities prevent them from admitting that failure was an integral part of their past. All successful athletes experience failure and provide a valuable service to their admirers by admitting to it as part of the educational experience we offer others. Failure is humbling so we can share our past experiences and teach others that there is no harm in early failure. Failure has a huge upside. One possible reason successful people do not admit to failure is arrogance. Smiley (2011) claims that the arrogant among us have the most to hide. To Smiley, arrogance is pretentious.

ARROGANCE IS FALSE MOTIVATION

Arrogance diminishes wisdom—Arabian proverb (Smiley, 2011, p. 7)

Let another man praise thee, and not thine own mouth; a stranger, and not thine own lips.—Proverbs 27:2

Arrogance is an important issue on the topic of motivation and failure because it is a personal characteristic of some people who try to hide their fear of failure and their history of actually experiencing failure; arrogance is the "great cover-up." Cover-up of what? Of deep-rooted insecurity. Arrogance manifests as bragging, bravado, self-serving behavior, and the appearance of superiority over others. Bravado masks insecurity, anxiety, and low self-esteem.

Arrogance helps the person overcompensate for feelings of emptiness, uncertainty, fear, and other undesirable thoughts and emotions. In sport, arrogant athletes and coaches want to be exalting themselves and give the appearance of patting themselves on the back, as a figure of speech. True leaders do not exalt themselves; effective leaders are exalted by their subordinates. An arrogant athlete does not give others space to celebrate who he or she is, to revel in that athlete's accomplishments. An arrogant athlete tells others about his or her accolades before others ever get a chance (Smiley, 2011). For these reasons, arrogance is always "ugly" and never a compliment to one's personality and behavior.

A study by Drs. Day and Silverman (1989) found a link between arrogance, poor job performance, and negativity on the job. The Workplace Arrogance Scale was used to determine if arrogance was related to job performance. They found that increased arrogance was associated with more self-centeredness and less agreeableness. In addition, arrogance had a significant negative effect on an organization's morale and profitability. Thus, there might be a competitive advantage in curtailing arrogant behavior in organizations and encouraging positive behaviors such as humility. To Smiley (2011), if arrogance is the disease, then humility is the cure. Humility is central to what is called "the power of purpose."

The concept of separating confidence and arrogance comes from a quote from National Football League Washington Redskins quarterback Robert Griffin III in a television interview. Are his words a demonstration of confidence or arrogance?

> I feel like I'm the best quarterback in the league, and I have to go out and show that. Any athlete at any level, if they concede to someone else, they're not a top competitor, they're not trying to be the best that they can be. There's guys in this league that have done way more than me. But I still view myself as the best, because that's what I work toward every single day. (Chase, 2015)

The argument in favor of categorizing this statement as confidence, not arrogance, is that Griffin is reflecting his feelings, and he is not indicating a sense of superiority over others. He claims to be the best, but he is not arrogant about it; he is not saying "I'm the best," but rather, "I have the required skills," no name-calling, no attempt to say anything at the expense of an opponent's self-esteem or questioning anyone else's competence. He says he tries to earn the recognition as "best quarterback" through hard work and diligence every day. That's a confident athlete. He has a strong sense of what is called "purpose."

THE POWER OF PURPOSE

What do we want in life (our vision) and how do we intend to obtain it (our mission)? What inspires us to set and attempt to meet goals that are meaningful and life changing? Like everyone else, athletes need inspiration to change certain areas of their life and to feel capable of performing at the highest level. How should sport participants expend and focus their energy in ways that are consistent with their deepest values and beliefs about what they consider really important? Instead of reacting to immediate needs and challenges, called expedient adaptation to immediate demands, how can we determine what is really important to us and what it will take to achieve and excel at the highest level—a process called values-based adaptation? What sacrifices in life are we willing to make to achieve our goals and be consistent with our values? This—the link between our core values and our actions—is what is called the *power of purpose*.

The power of purpose is about linking the athletes' most important values (e.g., family, health, faith, happiness, integrity/character, honesty, among many others) with their vision about where they want to go—what is meaningful in their life—and then to plan and complete their mission by determining their strategy or action plan. Coaches need to help their athletes identify their most important values and to define a vision, using a vision statement, for themselves about where they want to go, both personally and professionally. Developing a vision statement helps provide the energy needed to navigate obstacles and barriers, such as experiencing and dealing with failure in order to complete their mission.

PERSISTENCE

As indicated before, we do not learn and achieve without experiencing failure. Failure, by itself, is not the problem in our drive toward success. The problem is our *reaction* to failure. This is at the heart of persistence. We become paralyzed in using failure as a stepping-stone toward success without the ability to maintain focused in overcoming the array of obstacles that block our path. Many athletes are afraid to carry on after experiencing failure—at least as failure is defined by most athletes and their coaches.

Coaches, parents, and sport psychology consultants might consider communicating with the unhappy athlete in this way: "You struck out three times in today's game. What can you learn from that experience? Was the pitcher overpowering—just too difficult to hit—or do you feel that your batting skills need to improve? Were you thinking too much in the batter's box? Did you lack confidence in your ability to hit the ball? What do you think you need to work on and practice in order to improve your batting performance?" Persistence is clearly needed so that our experiences—successful and not successful—can be applied for future use and a better chance of success. Athletes must exhibit mental toughness in developing their strategy for handling failure, and persistence is at the heart of this strategy.

STOP MAKING EXCUSES

Excuses, if used to avoid taking responsibility for failure, often get in the way of finding the truth and learning from errors. Experiencing failure as a vehicle for improving sports performance means finding the true reasons for our mistakes and errors. It is unfair and demotivating for coaches or, for that matter, anyone in a supervisory position, to attribute failure to a lack of effort or low skill in the absence of factual information to support that contention. On the other hand, the athlete's tendency to avoid responsibility for undesirable performance outcomes is also damaging and prevents growth, learning, and performance improvement. Motivation is generated when athletes take responsibility for their performance, while at the same time, not being too self-critical. While self-blame can be harsh and inaccurate, just as damaging is the tendency to make excuses and not take responsibility for performance outcomes. We need to learn from experiences of failing.

CELEBRATE SUCCESS

A very strong source of motivation and confidence in sport is the athlete's perception of competence. Performing complex sport skills successfully, particularly under competitive conditions, is difficult to achieve and relatively rare. Failure (i.e., committing errors, making mistakes, losing) is far "easier" to experience and more common than success. Remember, successful baseball batting—a batting average of .300 or higher—consists of getting a hit (on base) only 3 out of 10 times. Therefore, when success is clearly experienced—performance outcomes are desirable—it is highly motivating to recognize and celebrate it. Plenty of training, skill building, practice, and coaching went into developing the ability to succeed. Recognizing a performer's competence is one of the components of building intrinsic motivation. The coach is the most credible source of information in sport, so this person must take responsibility for giving positive (success) information feedback.

Ultimately, motivation in competitive sport is about "failing better." We should not avoid failure, because we cannot improve without it. But each day we desire another chance to improve and use failure as a means to an end. Failure should be viewed as our constant companion; we thrive on it in order to reach our potential. Motivation provides the energy, focus, and satisfaction that lead to success. Motivation is the engine that generates the power and endurance needed to excel at the highest level consistently and efficiently. Motivation also breeds endurance, persistence, and adherence in preparing, carrying out, and completing the mission for sport success. The source of these processes starts within the athlete, but is monitored, coordinated, and initiated by the team's leader—the coach. High-quality leaders do not give in to failure; they rise above it. What separates great leadership from good intentions is the courage and commitment to stay the course, no matter how difficult the path.

Well-Known Entertainers Who Failed Before They Succeeded

Many people considered famous in English-speaking countries, especially the United States, began their respective careers being often rejected and as performance failures (from "50 Famously Successful People Who Failed at First," n.d.).

Jerry Seinfeld: The first time comedian Jerry Seinfeld appeared at a comedy club, he forgot his monologue and was booed until he finally left the stage. Seinfeld agreed he was terrible, but he also knew that he had "the right stuff" to get it right. He returned to the same club the next night, delivered his act with greater confidence, and received the laughter and applause he always expected. Even the best can fall in the beginning of their career.

Fred Astaire: After Astaire's first screen test, the testing director of MGM wrote, "Can't act. Can't sing. Slightly bald. Can dance a little." Astaire went on to become a highly successful actor, singer, and dancer.

Sidney Poitier: After this actor's first audition, Poitier was told by the casting director, "Why don't you stop wasting people's time and go out and become a dishwasher or something?" Poitier vowed to overcome this insult and went on to win an Oscar. He became one of the world's most well-respected actors.

Charlie Chaplin: The well-known comedian and film star Charlie Chaplin was initially rejected by Hollywood. They felt his act was a little too nonsensical and would never be accepted by the public. Chaplin eventually won the Lifetime Achievement Award from the film industry's Academy Awards.

Lucille Ball: During her career, Ball had 13 Emmy nominations and four wins, also earning the Lifetime Achievement Award from the Kennedy Center Honors. Before starring in the television show *I Love Lucy*, Ball was widely regarded as a failed, untalented actress. Even her drama instructors didn't feel she could make it, telling her to try another profession. She proved them all wrong.

Harrison Ford: In his first film, Ford was told by the movie execs that he simply didn't have what it takes to be a star. Today, Ford can proudly show that he does, in fact, have what it takes.

Marilyn Monroe: While Monroe died young, she did have a period of great success in her life. Despite a rough upbringing and being told by modeling agents that she should instead consider being a secretary, Monroe became a model and actress.

Oliver Stone: This Oscar-winning filmmaker and director began his first novel while at Yale, a project that eventually caused him to fail out of school. The novel was rejected by publishers. He enlisted in the army and fought in the Vietnam War, which inspired him to direct several high-quality films centered on war.

5

ERRORS LEAD TO OPTIMAL PERFORMANCE

Failure is success if we learn from it.

—Malcolm Forbes (Zoë B, 2013)

People are driven by numbers; improved changes in quantitative data motivate us. That is the central focus of this chapter; how numbers, specifically error detection and error corrections, can provide information that tells athletes (and their coaches) that performance is improving. It's about turning perceived failure into perceived success. Therefore, the purpose of this chapter is to establish the connection between performance error and failure, and how errors necessarily lead to achievement and success. This process is based on the concept of *positive failure*. Positive forms of failure start with learning from experience. It is not possible to learn in the absence of failure, particularly in the areas of detecting and correcting errors. While errors—in both physical and mental form—can lead to failure, performance failure is not always defined and dependent on making errors. An error is measurable and often (though not always) observable. Error, particularly if several are experienced quickly during a single event, can lead to performance failure.

Failure, itself, can be a function of unmet expectations and the lack of desirable outcome(s). The coach or athlete may explain a performance outcome as failure based on athletic performance that is short of meeting personal expectations rather than performing poorly. For example, an athlete can aim to achieve high-quality performance in sports competition, making 8 out of 10 free throws, a highly successful performance.

In academic settings, a student might earn an A in three out of four courses and a B in the fourth course. This student (or his or her parents) might categorize this outcome as failure, or at least "disappointing." Most individuals, however, would consider this outcome—three As and one B—highly desirable or successful.

There is an extensive body of applied research that integrates performance errors as a component of the process of learning and performing motor/sport skills. Learning concerns various techniques that separate accurate versus inaccurate, perfect from imperfect, optimal from suboptimal performance quality. Well-published motor learning scholar Dr. Robert Singer (1980) writes, "Is it better to learn with errors discouraged or encouraged? Can and should we learn from mistakes? Is it better to minimize the possibility of erroneous responses?" (p. 439).

Singer contends that learning a motor skill, what he calls "skilled motor performance," actually *requires*, or mandates, a learning phase. This phase consists of a smoothing out or coordinating the more observable aspects. He contends that skill cannot be defined in absolute terms, but rather is relative. Thus, skilled performance reflects the accumulation of error and what has resulted in a smoothing out or coordination of observable behavior. Consequently, what may be skilled performance in youth sport may not necessarily be considered skilled performance at more advanced levels. These groups differ by the degree and frequency of committing errors and producing successful performance outcomes. Error, in other words, is not only expected; it's necessary in the skill-building process.

There are many benefits of experiencing and responding to errors as building blocks in the process of achieving optimal performance. Making errors is central to building skills and achieving desirable performance outcomes. Errors lead to learning when they are first detected and then corrected. Error detection includes finding the benefit in every unpleasant or unsuccessful experience. Error correction occurs when the performer's efforts and outcomes are compared to others (i.e., inter-individual competition) or compared to one's previous best (i.e., intra-individual competition).

Sandy Koufax was a left-handed pitcher for the Los Angeles Dodgers baseball team in the early and mid-1960s. For the first six seasons of his professional career he struggled, trying to throw the baseball "through" his catcher—at very high velocity—rather than pitching to particular locations. He lacked ball control and was not targeted by the Dodgers as a future successful pitcher. He was on the bench for the first six seasons of his career. However, things turned around in 1961 when he learned to pitch properly and "hit his spots." He was notorious for pitching to a hitter's weakness. He said, "Pitching is the art of instilling fear [in the batter]," and "Show me a guy who can't pitch inside and I'll show you a loser" (Schwartz, n.d.).

Koufax went on to throw four no-hitters, earn three Cy Young Awards for best pitcher in the major leagues, and finish his career with an incredibly low 2.02 earned run average from 1962 to 1966. As All-Star Pittsburgh Pirates baseball player Willie Stargell said about Koufax, "Hitting against him is like eating soup with a fork" (Schwartz, n.d.). As a matter of integrity, Sandy Koufax retired at the young age of 30 due to finger and elbow injuries. According to his online profile, "When he knew he was damaged goods, *he* decided his career was over, not the Los Angeles Dodgers. At the peak of his game, Koufax simply walked away" (Schwartz, n.d.).

One elite athlete who thrived on overcoming errors and reaching the top of his position was baseball Hall of Famer and pitching great Sandy Koufax.

MEASURING ERROR

If error, the primary source of failure in sport, is to have a positive and important impact on the learning process, then we need to know the principles of measuring error. There are guidelines for determining procedures and criteria for measuring performance. These same guidelines can be used to measure failed outcomes and then apply the numbers to detect improved performance. The guidelines follow:

1. *Select the appropriate tasks* to measure learning and performance. Tasks should not be too complex. It is important to detect performance improvement. Tasks should also not be too easy, in which all

individuals experience significant improvement and there is a "ceiling effect" (i.e., all individuals reach their optimal performance level due to an over-easy task). Singer (1980) suggests "the task should be appropriate for the maturational level of the subjects" (p. 53).

2. *Determine the number of learning trials* as well as the time and equipment needed to collect performance data. When is task mastery determined? For instance, when does a basketball player master free-throw shooting?

3. *Select the type of performance score* (i.e., what researchers call the "dependent variable"). What and how will performance be measured? Is the data set quantitative (numbers driven for statistical analyses) or qualitative (comments and statements are categorized)? For instance, how many tennis serves fall within three feet of the targeted area? Most texts in the motor behavior area recognize the following scoring techniques: (a) Time required for completing each trial (attempt); (b) Number of errors committed during each trial; (c) the product of task completion time and number of errors per trial; and (d) the sum of completion time and number of errors per trial.

4. *Determine the learning score(s).* Has learning occurred? Is performance better? The athlete's scores must be specific and detailed to detect even small changes in the performance numbers, which will reflect improved skill (or fitness). This is why using wins and losses as the criteria to determine performance success, treatment effectiveness, or improved skill may be too broad and general. Think about using inches for the target of baseball bunting skills or accuracy of any striking skill. Performance and learning error must be sufficiently refined so that the desired outcome can be located and improvement noted, for instance, location of a volleyball serve. Did learning occur? Is the instructional technique or other intervention effective? What areas of the motor/sport task appear to improve, and which aspect(s) did not? What are the implications for athletes in future attempts and applying these skills in game conditions?

Sports fans and spectators are often critical of athletes who make errors or fail to achieve desired results. This is especially true in professional sports in which spectator expectations are especially high. Few spectators, however, have ever faced a major league pitch, and even fewer know how difficult it is to hit a pitched baseball traveling at 90 miles per hour. Motor behavior researcher Dr. Karl M. Newell (1974), while at the University of Illinois, conducted a scientific study on the speed of decision making while batting against a 90-mile-an-hour fastball. Journalist George F. Will (1990) put the findings in lay terms:

> A 90-mile-per-hour fastball that leaves a pitcher's hand 55 feet from the plate is traveling 132 feet per second and will reach the plate in .4167 seconds [under half a second]. A change-up or slow breaking ball loitering along at just 80 miles per hour travels 117.3 feet per second and will arrive in .4688 seconds. The difference is .052 of a second and is crucial. Having decided to try to hit the pitch, the batter has about two-tenths of a second to make his body do it. The ball can be touched by the bat in about 2 feet of the pitch's path, or for about fifteen-thousandths of a second. So, anyone who hits a ball thrown by a major league pitcher—who even just puts the ball in play—is doing something remarkable. The consistently good hitters are astonishing. (pp. 192–193)

In other words, the batter has to make his decision to swing or not swing before the pitch is halfway to the plate. This means the batter's mental approach should be to initiate a swing if he, in fact, intends to swing at the pitch, and then hold up—not swing—if the pitch is perceived as outside the strike zone. The skill of baseball batting is remarkably difficult; error is inevitable.

FORMS OF PERFORMANCE FEEDBACK

Learning and improving performance cannot occur in the absence of feedback—that is, information given to learners/athletes that points out the level of *quality* of the performed task and/or discloses the degree of success of the *outcome*. The type of feedback on *performance quality* is called *knowledge of performance* (KP), while feedback that reflects the degree of success based on *outcomes* is called *knowledge of results* (KR). Both types of feedback are needed to experience learning and to use failure as a stepping stone to improved performance.

Knowledge of Performance

Perhaps the most important function of feedback is providing error information that athletes can use to correct or refine their skills. Examples would be changing—or not changing—the release point of the athlete's throwing action, attempting to strike a ball in flight at a certain angle, or anticipating an opponent's movement and location on the court or field based on past performance tendencies.

KP can be delivered in either verbal or visual form. To reduce the information load for integrating feedback, athletes might be given what is called *summary feedback* or *average feedback*. Summary feedback reflects information about a subset, or brief, of trials or times that accurately reflects the athlete's overall level of performance quality. How effective was the offensive lineman during a football drill? How did the tennis player respond to his or her opponent's serves? How effective was the athlete bunting the ball in batting practice? Average feedback provides information about an accumulated set of trials over time that accurately provides an overall impression of performance quality and where, in particular, the skill needs to improve.

Knowledge of Results

KR, also called extrinsic/external/augmented/supplementary feedback, reflects performance outcomes and is usually *visually* observed. KR reflects the athlete's skill level in meeting performance goals. Perhaps the clearest example of KR is attempts to hit the bulls-eye in archery or some other aiming task that includes a specific visual target. Feedback is provided by an external source (teacher or coach) or through the learner's/athlete's own efforts. Ostensibly, the learner uses KR information in subsequent attempts.

It is important that KR be detailed and specific, but not too detailed, too specific, or offered too often. These guidelines address one fundamental limitation among subelite performance: information overload. Humans process information at variable rates of speed based on the complexity and amount of information entering the system in a given time period. Elite athletes can process a greater quantity and complexity of KR than nonelites due to the ability of elites to perform complex skills and subskills automatically with minimal thinking. Thus, elites can concentrate and focus their attention on selected aspects of the skill or strategy needed to improve performance under specific external conditions. For instance, how effectively can a tennis or badminton player anticipate his opponent's shots or a soccer player anticipate an opponent's dribbling and passing tendencies? Anticipation is an important mental strategy, especially at the elite level where high movement speed is so common.

A football receiver, for instance, can be told to run to a specific area, let's say 10 yards downfield, plant his right foot in the turf, and head toward midfield, and expect the ball (passed by the quarterback) to arrive at a certain location in time for making the catch. If the ball arrives too early or too late, the player and his coach need to examine where the movement error occurred, or whether the quarterback's throw was inaccurate. The receiver's footwork and other movements prior to making the catch are performed automatically so that the player can pick up other cues in the environment that might change the play pattern. Performance feedback, in the form of KP and KR, are essential to the motor learning process and should be incorporated in all practice situations in the skill learning process.

BAD LUCK: WHEN FAILURE ERRORS CANNOT BE EXPLAINED

Have you ever watched a fast-paced sporting event such as ice hockey, football, or basketball and noticed how a matter of inches—or less—separates success from failure? Or have you seen a hit baseball go foul by inches? Sport is about fractions of inches and milliseconds. A hockey puck can miss the net or bounce off a defender faster than human reaction time, which ranges from about .25 to .50 seconds. A hockey puck that is passed to a teammate can unintentionally miss the teammate's stick by an inch and, therefore, result in a missed opportunity to score a goal. Games are won or lost by a single point all the time.

Passing the ball in most sports inherently contains risk (error); however, coaches can try to minimize the degree of error by keeping passes short, creating plays and strategies that are low risk (relatively simple given the athletes' skill level and overlearning the skill so that it is executed with as little thinking as possible). Therefore, a ball or puck can miss its intended target by a very small degree and be considered an error when, in fact, the play was carried out flawlessly and, if repeated, would be successful (mistake free). What is considered failure may have nothing to do with skill level, strategy, an environmental condition, or a planned event. Performance outcome can simply reflect bad luck.

THE VALUE OF GOOD LUCK

In Chapter 3 the motivational advantages of explaining the causes of performance outcomes was examined. Generally speaking, attribution theory posits that high ability and effort explanations should follow *perceived* success, whereas task difficulty (e.g., "That was a very good opponent we played against today") and bad luck (e.g., "The ground ball took a bad hop and went over my glove") should be partial or full explanations of *perceived* failure (remember, *success* and *failure* are perceptions and outcomes, or end products). Life, however, is more complex than following general principles of behavior, especially when a person's actions are in response to external conditions and the actions of others. There is nothing wrong with using luck—either good or bad—as a way of interpreting and perceiving desirable performance outcomes when it is "the truth." But sometimes luck is actually desirable and used more often by highly skilled than less-skilled athletes. This narrative is reported by news and sports analyst George F. Will in his book on the craft of baseball (see box below).

"Professor Stephen Jay Gould of Harvard . . . argues that long (hitting or pitching) streaks necessarily are products of, are compounds of, skill and luck. Great athletes have a higher probability of success than normal athletes have in any instance—any at bat, any inning pitched. A streak is a series of discrete events occurring with the probability that is characteristic for a particular player at a particular point in his career. Frederick the Great, when asked what kind of generals he preferred, answered: 'Lucky ones.' He was, as was his wont, being serious. His point was that luck is unpredictable but talent takes advantage of it. Thus the talented have, in effect, more of it. It magnifies the tendencies of the talented. In the future, just over the horizon, in the next game, the next inning, the next at bat, there lurks something that can never be wholly subdued by talent or eliminated by training and preparation. That recurring thing is luck. . . . The ratio of talent to luck is high. But luck is part of the equation."—George F. Will (1990, p. 85)

LEARNING FROM MISTAKES AND FAILURE

Two central themes of this book are that failure is inevitable and that mistakes and errors are the building blocks of failure. What, then, is the process of learning from failure and mistakes? The main objective in addressing this issue is to learn to gain something from our losses. We need to develop strategies for learning from failure, for turning losses into profits. These are the questions that need answers:

1. What or who was the cause of the failure? What went wrong? As objectively as possible, try to find the root of the problem so that it can be addressed in future situations. What can and cannot be controlled in future situations? What is your strategy to minimize the chance of a repeated failure situation?

2. Was the event actual failure or bad luck? Were there unrealistic expectations of success? Were there temporary conditions (e.g., bad weather, poor play calling, superior opponent, bad luck) that led to the problem? What did not work? Did someone have unrealistic expectations? (Unrealistic) thoughts of perfection?

3. Can you discover components within the failed experience you can label successes? What went well? What do you want to see transferred to the next occasion?

4. What lessons can be learned from what happened? If the bigger and heavier ball of snow is not at the lowest location on the snowman, the structure will collapse. We learn to put the largest ball of snow at the bottom of the snowman to act as a foundation for the second and third (smaller) balls of snow. When we don't leave home with a hat or umbrella when the weather is threatening or raining, we get wet and very uncomfortable. It's all about having a positive attitude toward the main goal of making mistakes—learning.

5. Ask yourself, "How can I be grateful for the failed experience?" It is important to feel gratitude and to appreciate the learning outcomes of the experience. We do not win every game, never make physical or mental errors, and always fall short of reaching our expectations in sport. But if we learned that this pitcher throws a good curveball when he or she should be throwing a fastball on that pitch count,

next time we will look for the curve and appreciate the opportunity for that discovery.

6. How can my failure become successes? Are there any actual benefits from this failed experience? If you lost your concentration minutes before the race and became intimidated by an opponent who runs a faster race, practice avoiding this limitation before the next race. It takes concentration and other mental skills to be a successful athlete, in this case, a sprinter.

7. Who else can help you learn from mistakes? We all need a support system. In sport, we have coaches, teammates, parents (especially for younger athletes), sport psychologists (also called a mental skills coach), predecessors, friends, and perhaps the occasional informal observer. We need to learn from the mistakes of others and seek advice from those who have successfully handled failure.

8. Finally, what happens next? There needs to be an *action plan* that helps us focus on the future. Learning is defined as a *permanent* change in behavior. What permanent changes are you prepared to make, and when? What else do you need to ensure these changes? Then do it! The failure to carry out an action plan may be due to defensiveness, arrogance, or the perception of not having enough time. Avoid these characteristics, remain humble, and plow ahead with the increased knowledge and technique needed to overcome repeated failure.

A TEACHER RESIGNS DUE TO FAILURE-FREE SCHOOL GRADING SYSTEM

Sometimes educators, who should know better, think that failure should be avoided at all costs. The following is an actual letter to the editor that appeared in the *Daily News Journal* (Tennessee), written by a teacher who resigned her high school teaching position due to administrative decisions that did not permit students to fail.

To the editor, I am writing to all of my students and parents who have supported me over the past nine years at [LaVergne High School in Tennessee]. Recently I had to make a very tough decision to resign my position as a math teacher. I wanted to tell you why I decided to leave. I became a teacher to make a difference, and I believe I succeeded with a lot of students. I have always expected my students to put forth an effort and work hard to learn. Not only did my students learn how to do algebra, they learned how to be confident in their own abilities. Some of my students had to fail first to realize how important success was. My students definitely had to practice in order to master algebra. When I found out I couldn't count homework as a grade and my students couldn't fail, it was like the most important tools of teaching were being taken away. Can a contractor build a house without tools? Parents, be aware of what your children are doing in school. If your child brings home an "A" in a class, question what he/she learned. I know that kids who earn their grades by working hard will go on to be more successful in life than those who are given a grade for doing nothing. We have enough people in our country who expect something for nothing . . . ("A Teacher Resigns," 2010, p. B2)

In summary, at the heart of performance failure are error, physical and mental mistakes, and unmet expectations. The coach is in a position to use failure experiences to benefit the athlete. Fitness instructors can provide performance feedback to improve exercise technique and fitness outcomes. Feedback should be offered that is specific and detailed in content, timely, ongoing (consistent but not constant), and informative. Perhaps most important of all is that failure be perceived as an opportunity for personal growth and development, and improving the probability for future success.

6

PROPER COPING
WITH FAILURE

*My great concern is not whether you have failed, but whether you
are content with failure.*

—Abraham Lincoln (Zoë B, 2013)

Failure is inevitable in competitive sport, no matter how it is defined and/
or acknowledged. Athletes make physical and mental errors, injuries are
experienced, sports officials make "bad" calls, and opponents are sometimes
successful. The result is experiencing stress in both acute (sudden) and
chronic (prolonged) forms. In addition, each of these sources of stress and
each stressful experience is interpreted by athletes at various intensity levels.
It is the athlete's *reactions* to these stressful experiences that require specific
coping skills to reduce their harmful mental, emotional, and physical effects.

If failure in sport is inevitable, so are stressful experiences. The process
of preventing or managing stress in reducing its intensity and frequency is
called *coping*. Coping is usually defined as a person's conscious attempt to
use psychological or behavioral ways to manage or reduce acute (sudden)
or chronic (long-term) stress. The proper use of coping strategies includes
using mental and behavioral techniques that help athletes *manage stress*
(i.e., mental or physiological responses to an immediate event interpreted as

undesirable and threatening) and *anxiety* (i.e., thoughts of worry and threat about a future event or situation, often accompanied by unpleasant thoughts and physiological processes such as sweating, tense muscles, and increased respiration rate).

While many individuals view the concept of coping as an indication of effective responses to stress, nothing can be further from the truth. Coping is a skill and may or may not be used effectively. Ineffective coping is evident in violent (usually illegal) reactions to stressful events, receiving penalties during the contest, being removed from the contest by the game official, taking mind-altering drugs, and using tobacco and other unhealthy actions. As this chapter points out, experiencing sport stress and adversity has several benefits when it comes to experiencing failure in sport.

BENEFITS OF ADVERSITY

Adversity, defined in most dictionaries as "misfortune" or "a troubled state," is good—even necessary—in order to achieve at the highest level. As J. C. Maxwell (2000) writes, "The process of achievement comes through repeated failures and the constant struggle to climb to a higher level" (p. 133). There are numerous benefits of experiencing adversity:

1. *Adversity creates resilience.* Concepts related to resilience include resourcefulness, mental toughness, and hardiness. They all reflect a disposition that allows athletes to persevere under duress—stress, anxiety, and negative moods—and in response to challenges. Adversity is similar to the training outcomes from weight lifting. Overcoming resistance as part of the weight training process results in bigger, more efficient muscles. This is because muscle fibers tear during the lifting process. Repair of each fiber consists of a process called protein synthesis, which increases the diameter of each muscle fiber. The result is an increase in the size of muscles used in that specific exercise. In sport, athletes become more resilient to the emotional challenges of competition.

2. *Adversity develops maturity.* High-quality sports performers have become wise by experiencing failure. Some of our brightest minds, successful entrepreneurs, and elite athletes have failed repeatedly

during their journey to achieve. For example, author George Will (1990) reports on the past performance failures of numerous baseball managers as players, but who have been among the most successful managers. Will contends that "a lot of excellent managers were marginal players. . . . In modern times, mediocre playing careers have been the preludes to some of the most distinguished managerial careers" (p. 26). An example, according to Will, is former highly successful baseball manager Tony La Russa, who "was a mediocre player." Other examples of highly successful baseball managers with a poor-performing playing career include Earl Weaver (Baltimore Orioles), Sparky Anderson (Cincinnati Reds and Detroit Tigers), and Whitey Herzog (St. Louis Cardinals).

It takes a great deal of tenacity combined with the maturity of knowing one's potential to reach one's future, challenging goals. We become wiser by experiencing adversity.

3. *Adversity expands our capacity to perform at the highest level.* We tend to perform better when our back is against the wall, and we are under some degree of stress. We do not perform at optimal levels when the task is easy and we are not under duress. We expand our capacity to perform, increase confidence, and build skills under conditions of turmoil and uncertainty. The chance of failure forces us to plan and rethink our future actions.

4. *Adversity promotes opportunities to reach our potential.* A number of high school and college students apply for particular academic programs that are intended to promote their professional training and expertise. But sometimes those plans change by a school rejection, and the student must find interest in a different program and profession. Sometimes athletes try out for a specific sports team but don't make it. Their athletic careers are suddenly changed or terminated, and they are then forced to choose a different direction in life. My dream of entering professional baseball was cut short by competing against other student athletes with bigger physical stature and superior talent, so instead of pursuing a baseball career I gave 100% toward my undergraduate degree and went on to obtain master's and doctoral degrees in movement science in preparation for a career in higher education. Sometimes things work out for the best.

5. *Adversity prompts innovation.* To create something new requires trust in one's ability and energy. Most inventors of our modern technology—including the light bulb, the telephone, and the computer—all failed repeatedly until more knowledge was acquired with each attempt. Finally, after dozens, even hundreds, of failures these magnificent inventions came to life. Dealing with failure—adversity—created our modern world.

6. *Adversity is motivational.* There is nothing like feeling your back is against the wall and that your destiny may not be reached due to adversity. This condition is the antecedent of anxiety; thoughts of worry about some future event, feeling threatened about unpleasant and unplanned experience, lack of self-control in regulating the situation, and not knowing the outcome. Elite athletes—and their coaches—spend an excessive amount of time planning for all scenarios that may occur during the contest. They always ask the question, "What if . . . ?" They have a primary plan (Plan A) and a secondary plan (Plan B, which is also called "What if . . . ?"). Competing against an opponent perceived as superior or at least well skilled is highly motivating to elite-level performers. Their self-esteem, ability, sport skills, and reputation are all on the line; failure is not an option. Yes, adversity is highly motivational for athletes who have a strong need to achieve and plan on being successful.

Adversity in sport is a necessary component of failure, and yet failure helps a person directly deal with the barriers that come with adversity. Failure has value, and that value is in the form of information, learning, and improving one's performance. An athlete learns from experience that adversity has great potential to enable him or her to reach optimal performance and to challenge his or her physical limits toward successful outcomes. One set of skills that must be learned as part of dealing with adversity is coping.

COPING WITH SPORT STRESS AND ADVERSITY

Highly effective coping skills must follow failure, even at the elite level, to deal with the stress that comes from failure. Although avoiding adversity and stress in sport is highly desirable, that option is not realistic. The process of sport competition inherently leads to failure, and failure can be stressful, requiring the use of coping strategies. The question is not to determine ways to avoid stress, adversity, and anxiety in sport, but how to deal (cope) with it effectively. How do the best athletes cope effectively? To best understand ways to cope with failure in sport we need to briefly review the coping process.

THE COPING PROCESS

The coping process in sport consists of stages that the athlete goes through in his or her thoughts (called cognition) or feelings (called emotion) in response to experiencing stress. Feeling stress consists of how we interpret events and the causes of those events. Dropping a ball, causing a performance error, is not necessarily stressful unless the athlete, and perhaps the coach, categorizes that experience as stressful. A dropped ball that occurs in practice may be interpreted as bad luck, a learning experience, or simply not stress (i.e., benign, harmless). However, a dropped ball during the contest may be considered stressful if it places the team at a disadvantage and in danger of losing. Thus, events by themselves are not stressful; however, the interpretation of the event might be categorized as stressful.

How does the process of coping relate to failure in sport? First, similar to stress, failure is a perception; a label. And perceived failure is associated with low skills and other undesirable feelings that may not accurately reflect the athlete's level of competence. Losing a sports contest may be considered failure, at least as compared to winning. The *cause* of losing, however, may be more important than the actual outcome when using the label *failure*. Every year and during the season professional athletes try out and get cut from professional sport teams. So do athletes of all ages and skill levels. Are these athletes failures? Yes, if they demonstrated a lack of competence, but no, they are not failures, if they competed against someone with superior skills. They did their best and, as it turned out, someone else was judged (subjectively by an authority figure, perhaps a sports journalist) superior in meeting the team's needs. That does not appear to fit the criteria for failure. Let's examine the coping process so we can deal with failure more productively.

The coping process experienced very rapidly in this sequence:

1. The athlete experiences an event or detects a stimulus that enters the information processing system. For example, a tennis serve either lands in bounds ("return the ball") or out of bounds ("let the ball go; do not return the serve").
2. The stimulus or event is interpreted, or appraised, as stressful (i.e., challenging or threatening)—or not stressful. Other (nonstressful) appraisals may include that the event is harmless or even positive/beneficial. If we make a stress appraisal instead of appraisals called harmless or positive, we need to enact one or more coping strategies.

   Stress is an integral and constructive part of experiencing failure. Failure experiences, however, do not have to be stressful if we appraise the experience as challenging or even positive. For example, a football player who allows his opponent to overpower him—a stressful appraisal—learns that he must be faster and stronger on given plays, resulting in a *challenge stress appraisal*. A baseball pitcher struck the batter out on a curveball; next time the batter will remember the pitcher is capable of throwing a curveball for a strike even with three balls.
3. The third stage, assuming a stressful appraisal, is the proper use of coping skills. If the athlete makes nonstress appraisals, then no coping is needed. A stress appraisal, however, requires the use of effective coping strategies to reduce or manage the stressor's persistence and intensity level to promote optimal performance. Proper coping skills improve a person's ability to deal with and react to failure. The type of coping strategy used often depends on the situation but also the athlete's comfort level in applying a particular coping strategy that has been used effectively in the past. Conditions that require the use of approach and avoidance coping have been established in the literature.

APPROACH AND AVOIDANCE COPING WITH FAILURE IN SPORT

Coping strategies have been placed and studied according to different categories. One set of categories that has received extensive attention in the sport coping literature is called approach-avoidance coping. *Approach coping* strategies following sudden stress deal directly with the stressor and maintaining control of the stressful event. Examples include planning, seeking information, labeling an unpleasant situation (e.g., "The official was wrong on that call"), complaining, visualization, analyzing, and acts of aggression, all for the purpose of reducing stress intensity. *Avoidance coping* concerns conscious attempts to reduce or eliminate stressful feelings by not attending to input and processing of information, and then moving forward with the next task at hand. Visual distractors are ignored or filtered out. When a basketball player feels he was fouled but the referee misses that call, he can argue with the referee (approach coping) at the risk of the other team keeping the ball in play and scoring, or he can continue to compete and worry about the missed foul later, and at that time talk to the referee, if needed (avoidance coping). Sample avoidance coping strategies include prayer, attending to the next task/play at hand, not thinking about the stressful event immediately after it occurred, and mentally distancing oneself from the situation by ignoring the person (the source of stress).

How do—or should—athletes cope with failed performance? Highly skilled athletes use a variety of coping techniques, both mental (thoughts) and behavioral (actions). Using approach or avoidance coping depends on the type of stressful event the person is experiencing. Stressors that occur in situations that the athlete considers controllable, such as making an error or not carrying out the team strategy properly, usually result in approach coping; the athlete can do something about the problem. Less controllable stressful events, such as a bad call from the referee, superior performance by the opponent, or just bad luck, usually warrant avoidance coping. Also, sometimes there is time to use a coping skill, while other times the game is ongoing and there is no time.

For example, what can you do if the umpire calls a strike when the batter considers the pitch a ball? Not very much, other than to question the umpire and then move on and prepare for the next pitch, according to most sports organizations. If the defense missed a tackle in football and it was bad luck, again avoidance coping is best. If, however, the opponent shows a particular strategy that warrants a reaction, then approach coping—confronting the sources of stress—is needed. The use of a particular coping strategy can be categorized as effective or ineffective based on the situation (see Table 6.1),

Table 6.1. Coping Strategies Categorized by Dimensions, Subdimensions, and an Additional List of Ineffective Coping

Approach-Behavior Coping	Approach-Cognitive Coping
Confronting, threatening, arguing, information seeking, social support, explaining, discussing, catastrophizing, speaking to a mentor or coach, receiving counseling, soliciting opinions from others.	Covert rehearsal, planning, analyzing, self-talk reanalyzing, justifying, psyching-up, praying (if related to coping with a stressful situation), self-statements, friendly nonverbal/verbal logic/reason.
Avoidance-Behavior Coping	**Avoidance-Cognitive Coping**
Walking away, social engineering (avoiding a certain location), exercising, reading, watching television, listening to music, attending church, ingesting an alcoholic beverage, engaging in recreational activity, engaging in sexual behavior, playing or watching sports, reading, target shooting.	Discounting, psychological distancing, labeling, empathy, thought stopping, ignoring, self-talk, mental imagery, progressive relaxation, focusing on the next task, praying (if focusing on the Lord and not on the stressor).
Examples of Ineffective/Maladaptive Approach and Avoidance Coping	
Excessive alcohol, smoking, mind-altering drugs, emotional eating, prolonged anger and hostility, car speeding, drinking and driving (high risk taking), thoughts of self-destructive actions, negative self-talk, rumination (repeating self-blame), resignation (helplessness/hopelessness), exhibiting bad mood toward others, excessive exercise (also called exercise dependence).	

with some strategies more effective than others based on the type of stressor, the stressed individual's personality and usual manner of coping, and the costs versus benefits of coping in a certain manner—the cost-benefit ratio.

How should athletes cope with success? Wait, is this a typo? Do athletes really need to *cope* with success? Don't they *celebrate* success and relish their achievements? Is success stressful? Glad you asked: Yes, success can lead to stress and maladaptive (ineffective) coping. A good example of this apparent oxymoron comes from Michael Phelps, winner of multiple Olympic gold medals in swimming (see page 73).

Do elite athletes use one type of coping skill more than the other? The answer is "yes," *elite (successful) players tend to use avoidance coping more effectively than their non-elite peers*; putting the stressor behind you (i.e., avoidance coping) seems to be more difficult due to heightened emotions and the tendency to react aggressively (approach) to the stressor, when in

In 2004 swimming champion Michael Phelps won a record-breaking eight medals—six gold, two bronze—in the Olympic Games in Athens. But he was not through competing. He trained hard and won eight gold medals in swimming at the 2008 Olympics in Beijing.

After Beijing, Phelps contemplated retirement for the first time. How did he cope with the stress of an inactive, noncompetitive future? Poorly. He claimed to have nothing left to do. He did nothing for a long time and was not motivated to move in a new direction in life. He questioned his future path. Sadly, photos of Phelps smoking marijuana surfaced in the media, and his sponsors abandoned him. A subsequent arrest for driving drunk (DUI) made matters worse. The USA Swimming Association, which is the governing body for competitive swimming in the United States, suspended him for 3 months. Phelps was suffering from too much pressure and too much fame. To deal with his stress he used (ineffective) avoidance-behavioral coping—the use of drugs and alcohol—which almost ruined his career and his life. Then his life turned around, due in part to his coach, who instilled in him the need to keep swimming and to become the person—and swimmer—he used to be. He began training for the 2012 Olympics in London. He claimed that for the first time he just wanted to have fun training and competing in London. It was a wake-up call when he lost the first race—placing fourth. But he came back to win several additional medals. When he finally retired, Phelps had won a total of 27 medals for swimming, 18 of which were gold.

At what level was Phelps's commitment to being an Olympic champion? In the year leading up to the Athens Olympic Games in 2004, Phelps took just one day off from training—including weekends—and that one day was due to having his wisdom teeth removed. Michael Phelps loved to compete and hated to lose (Phelps & Cazeneuve, 2012).

fact, sometimes it is best to let it go and not get caught up in the stressful event. (The textbox on page 74 highlights a few well-known individuals who went from failure to life-changing success and had a significant influence on the world.) As we have already seen in this chapter, however, athletes (e.g., Michael Phelps) sometimes use maladaptive avoidance coping such as marijuana use, overeating, and excessive alcohol consumption. Phelps ended up being cited for DUI, but when he focused on returning to training for the next Olympic Games, an approach-behavioral coping strategy, he was able to overcome his boredom and lack of focus in life.

Inventors Who First Failed then Changed the Modern World

The following examples come from "50 Famously Successful People Who Failed at First" (n.d.).

Thomas Edison: As a young man, Edison was told by his teachers that he was "too stupid to learn anything." He was also fired from his first two jobs because employers found him nonproductive. Edison, however, proved to be tenacious and to believe in his own skills. He made over 1,000 unsuccessful attempts at inventing the lightbulb. To most people, he failed over 1,000 times, but Edison had a different interpretation; he claimed that he learned how *not* to invent the lightbulb over 1,000 times.

Orville and Wilbur Wright: The Wright brothers, inventors of the first airplane, started a bicycle shop that would play an important role in early attempts at flight. After several years of hard work and numerous failed attempts, while battling depression, the Wright brothers finally successfully tested the first airplane in 1903.

In summary, athletes are highly prone to experience failure because that is the nature of sports competition; someone wins and someone loses. Losing is considered failure by most sports participants. It is what occurs *after* failure, however, that leads to skill development, personal growth, and long-term success. Sports competition is also inherently stressful, in which athletes experience both chronic (e.g., team relationship and communication issues) and acute forms (e.g., making an error, receiving a bad call from the official, injury or pain). The process of preventing or overcoming sport stress is called coping. Each segment of the coping process is a skill and, like any skill, requires practice and time to master. Coping with failure is an inherent part of sport competition and the focus of this chapter. Categories of coping are designated as *approach* and *avoidance* in this chapter. Effective coping in sport, then, is an essential part of both preventing and using failure outcomes as a way to improve and master sport skills, and to achieve optimal performance.

Perhaps one of the most common coping methods used by highly skilled athletes is called cognitive reappraisal, in which stressed athletes interpret the stressful event in a new way. For instance, instead of perceiving the stressful event as harmful and threatening, athletes feel confident in their ability to learn from the situation and maintain high expectations about future success (Anshel, Kang, & Meisner, 2010). The combination of confidence, mental toughness, and high expectations about future performance among skilled athletes make cognitive reappraisal a frequent and effective coping technique. As the late writer and poet Oscar Wilde (1854–1900) is quoted as saying, "Believe in yourself and there will come a day when others will have no choice but to believe with you" (Esar, 1968, p. 712). Despite setbacks that result in errors, mistakes, failure, and even the lack of emotional support from others, it is essential to anticipate future success and consistently give 100% toward better future outcomes.

7

LINKING EFFECTIVE SPORTS LEADERSHIP TO FAILURE

Remember that failure is an event, not a person.

—Zig Ziglar, American author, salesman,
and motivational speaker (Zoë B, 2013)

No person experiences more failure than sports coaches or leaders in positions of authority (e.g., corporate managers and supervisors, educators, researchers, parents). Effective leaders must overcome adversity at every step. Overcoming adversity is the foundation of sports competition. This chapter will address how sports coaches should respond to their teams'—and their own—failure. Failure among coaches, not unlike other areas of practice, may be *perceived* or *actual* in meeting their own and others' performance expectations.

Examples of perceived failure in sports coaching include the athlete or team not performing better than the competition, either temporarily or permanently. Examples of temporary failure include undesirable performance outcomes within the contest, physical errors, mental errors, errors in decision making, poor planning, lack of anticipation during performance, competing unsuccessfully against a superior opponent, use of the wrong or an ineffective game strategy, poor use of coping skills following stressful contest-related experiences, and poor communication between coach and players. Examples of permanent failure include losing the contest, receiving a penalty of game dismissal, or persistent poor performance during the contest.

This chapter will address the following issues related to how sports coaches and others in leadership positions should (1) create a safe team/ player environment in which to fail; (2) operationally define *failure* to subordinates; (3) inform athletes why failure should, at times, actually be *encouraged*; (4) create a team atmosphere that promotes value and positive outcomes from failure; (5) provide cognitive (mental) and behavioral (observable) strategies in preparing for and handling (coping with) failure; (6) build desirable dispositions in handling failure, such as mental toughness, confidence, hardiness, and resourcefulness; and finally, (7) list undesirable characteristics of sports coaches who actually, often unwittingly, *contribute* to the athlete's failure and inhibit desirable performance outcomes (e.g., creating heightened athlete anxiety, inducing negative emotional intensity, exhibiting an uneven temperament and chronic anger, making wrong causal explanations of performance outcomes [e.g., "We were lucky" after success], and lacking compassion toward players and other team members). The results of ineffective coaching (leadership) qualities include the athlete's mental distraction, loss of concentration, inaccurate or poor decision making, and undesirable athletic performance quality.

CREATING A SAFE ENVIRONMENT TO FAIL

An environment that includes messages of the benefits of failure allows employees—and their superiors—the security to take risks. As Thomas Watson Sr., former IBM president, has reportedly said to the media, the fastest way to succeed is to double your failure rate. Successful business leaders have known for years that failure is a prerequisite to invention. Businesses have to encourage risk taking and learn from making mistakes. While failure by taking risks and errors are never desirable, these experiences are inevitable if companies—or sports teams and their athletes—go to the edge. For many individuals at the elite level of their profession, mistakes can mean losing money, the chance of promotion, and even a job (e.g., in sport, being cut from the team or experiencing a change in team status, from starter to non-starter; being dismissed as the team coach). On a personal level, making mistakes can cause embarrassment, result in loss of confidence in one's ability to lead, and lower likelihood of being hired elsewhere.

Creating an environment in which the players feel safe to fail consists of strong coach encouragement to players to take reasonable risks, not punishing or disciplining risk takers, providing detailed and informative feedback after performance errors, and praising athletes for taking risks.

The strategy for creating an environment that ensures a "soft landing," worker job security, safety, and compassion in response to failure is to make a deliberate, well-planned effort that makes failure desirable. This set of characteristics describes the failure-tolerant leader.

FAILURE-TOLERANT LEADERS

In the corporate world, Richard Farson and Ralph Keyes (2002) define *failure-tolerant leaders* as executives who, through their words and behavior, assist subordinates to successfully overcome their fear of failure and simultaneously create a culture of intelligent risk taking. The result, they predict, is long-term, persistent innovation. Rather than be protective of their power and defensive about their decisions—both good and bad—failure-tolerant leaders actually *encourage* failure. In competitive sport, failure-tolerant coaches motivate their athletes to go beyond simplistic, traditional definitions of failure, such as making errors or losing. They do not support the view that failure is the opposite of success, but rather, failure *complements* success. Innovation cannot occur unless the athlete takes risks.

Failure-tolerant coaches also analyze the cause(s) of mistakes rather than reflecting a sense of disapproval. They categorize mistakes into *excusable* and *inexcusable*. Excusable mistakes are outcomes that require further, in-depth examination to understand the causes of failure. In a sport context, the coach may question an athlete's preparation for the game, seek information about some mental aspect of competition (e.g., concentration, confidence, mastery of information about an opponent's tendencies), determine the presence of excessive mental or physical fatigue, or schedule more practice time to master a particular sport skill.

Failures that are the result of sloppiness or should have resulted in success but did not—inexcusable errors—also have to be analyzed. These "unwarranted" failures may cause greater concern toward the athletes' or team's skills, level of preparation, knowledge about technique, and motivation to prevent future failure outcomes. This is especially the case if the same errors and failure outcomes are made repeatedly.

Another characteristic of the failure-tolerant sports coach is their willingness to show interest, express support, and ask pertinent questions such as "What can I do to be a better coach—for you?" or "Based on your experience guarding number 55, how can we beat him to the basket?" These coaches take a genuine interest in their athletes' work and skill development. Rather than evaluating their efforts, these coaches try to understand the problems and challenges associated with being successful and avoiding failure.

Failure is more inevitable in sport environments that are threatening and tense. Too much of the athlete's energy is spent coping with the stress of a coach's anger and, instead, should be directed toward task-related athlete behaviors for achieving desirable performance outcomes. For example, instead of trying to avoid a confrontation with a coach or getting the coach upset due to asking a question or seeking information, athletes should be told by their coaches "There is no such thing as a stupid question." This statement informs each team member that it's better to know and properly use information than pretend to know all the answers, but get it wrong and make mistakes that might cost the team a victory.

Acknowledging to team members that failure has—or *can* have—very *positive* properties will help them focus on making better decisions, taking appropriate risks and initiatives, establishing more positive and supportive relationships with colleagues, and creating more energy in the sport environment. The athletes will be far less distracted with redundant or irrelevant environmental features and will not waste energy on negative emotions. The result will be improved concentration, faster and more accurate processing of external information, and better performance quality.

CREATING A "SAFE" ENVIRONMENT IN WHICH TO FAIL

Very few outcomes that fall below expectations should be labeled a failure. If these outcomes *are* considered failures, then the athletes need to know they are safe failures; everyone learns and improves from these experiences.

How is creating a "fail-safe" environment accomplished? The process begins with communication between coach and athlete. Nothing replaces hearing the coach say, in person and directly to the athlete(s), "Failure—either by individual athletes or by the entire team—can be a good thing, but under one condition: we learn from it and improve." If players hear *and* *believe* their coach condones failure as potentially helpful and constructive, the environment will be enriched by learning and playing better over time. Here are a few guidelines on creating a fail-safe sport environment:

1. Information feedback must be given to all team members, not just to starters or any other segment of the team. Include nonstarters in learning sessions; they also need to know they are relevant members of the team.
2. The information content should be specific and detailed so that athletes can apply it.
3. Information should be positive as well as instructive and critical ("What happened during the game that made you feel good and you want to see happen again?").
4. Feedback content should not be sarcastic or address the player's character or personality (i.e., avoid name-calling or sarcasm; stick with issues that can be observed and addressed).
5. The coach should not offer feedback at the same time he or she is upset. Athletes will filter out all feedback, much of it very important, due to their anxiety—feeling worried or embarrassed—when coaches openly display their negative feelings.
6. Never humiliate the athlete in front of teammates or spectators. It is fine to deliver feedback during a contest if it's brief, confidential, and in private.

In summary, failure-tolerant coaches clearly indicate to their teams that constructive mistakes are acceptable and worthwhile. Athletes feel that they have a "green light" to explore new possibilities, options, and strategies for reaching optimal performance. Instead of thinking in terms of success or failure, successful athletes consider their mistakes as learning experiences and as opportunities for improvement. Mistakes are viewed for their educational power and their potential to expand one's capacity to go beyond previous best performance. Failure is not feared; it's recognized, accepted, and praised.

OPERATIONALLY DEFINE "FAILURE" TO SUBORDINATES

An operational definition reflects the unique way a word or concept is used given certain situational characteristics and conditions. The word—and concept—of failure falls into the category of an operational definition because it means different things to different people and it differs from situation to situation. This is especially crucial for helping athletes understand the constructive and beneficial nature of failing in sport.

Is it failure when a baseball player gets two hits out of four attempts, a game batting average of .500? Is it failure for a baseball pitcher to throw a ball outside the strike zone, even four times with one batter, causing a walk? How high must a coach's or parent's expectations be in judging the athlete's level of performance? Should we expect our athletes to perform flawlessly? Should we expect and demand perfection? Is failure, therefore, the outcome of imperfection? If humans are inherently (genetically) imperfect, is it proper to compare human sport performance with the display of perfectly executed skills?

Failure is defined by most "experts," scholars, and writers as a *perception*, that is, an interpretation of a person's actions in a particular situation, condition, or event in comparison to actions in the same situation, condition, or event that are judged as successful, competent, or desirable. Failure is subjective; a judgment in the eye of the beholder. What determines whether the action was a failure? According to author John C. Maxwell (2000), *"You* are the only person who can really label what you do as a failure. It's subjective. Your perception of and response to your mistakes determines whether your actions are failures" (p. 17).

WHY FAILURE SHOULD BE ENCOURAGED

The suggestion that sports coaches, athletes, and parents of athletes should actually promote failure seems, on the surface, absurd. Why fail on purpose? Well, what if failure is really the beginning segment of success, and not really failure at all? While athletes are coached to avoid failure at all costs, the fact is that in sport *failure is good*—or at least has the potential to benefit the athlete. The central issue is not performing perfectly; that's not possible. Instead, the central issue is how we can learn from our shortcomings and errors. Why should failure be encouraged, not so much as an end in itself (i.e., "I failed so I guess I should not be playing this game . . .") but as a means to an end (i.e., "I should have been in the right position on that play and have to concentrate harder next time")?

Like anything else, failure has to be kept in perspective. The big picture is that mistakes—errors, performance limitations, poor judgment, inaccurate decision making, lack of anticipation—are a means to better performance, but only if high-quality feedback from physical and mental errors is provided to athletes by coaches or other observers. It is the assessment of performance technique and strategy that is so central to experiencing the advantages of failure. Thus, the coach needs to create a failure-friendly team atmosphere that promotes positive outcomes, particularly following failure.

THE ROLE OF EMPATHY IN LEARNING FROM MISTAKES

Perhaps the key concept that promotes the coach's acceptance of failure in sport is *empathy*. Champions fail as sports competitors, as do others, who try and try again to find the right mixture of ingredients for excellence. A top-rated researcher might say, "I failed with each attempt but the last one." Failures are like practice trials. It's not a disgrace to fail, and you must analyze each failure to find its cause. You must learn how to fail "intelligently." Athletes should "fail forward" toward success.

Coaches are most empathetic toward athletes when they (coaches) demonstrate and publicize their own missteps, mistakes in judgment, and fallibility in learning their position. For example, billionaire Bill Gates, creator of our original computer software packages, was a college dropout. Many scholars with extensive records of research suffered numerous failing grades in elementary and secondary school. Failure has been intrinsic to the successes of most high-quality sports performers. Athletes in virtually all sports underperformed before going on to have stellar sports careers. Examples include baseball greats Willie Mays, Hank Aaron, Mickey Mantle, and Ernie Banks, all of whom had initial baseball batting averages in the low 200s before eventually becoming all-stars and members of baseball's Hall of Fame. Early unpleasant experiences and struggles often work in the athlete's best interests by providing the incentive to work hard and not give up. To paraphrase former Chief Operating Officer of Procter and Gamble, A. G. Lafley, good leaders praise failure (Dillon, 2011).

PROVIDING PROPER FAILURE FEEDBACK

Failure is desirable only if the performer links failed attempts with feedback. When a person receives information about a failed experience, learning occurs; performance is eventually improved. In the following chapter, in the section called Coaching Strategies to Prevent and Overcome Failure, techniques for giving proper feedback following failure that the performer will interpret as constructive and positive are described. These techniques include the Sandwich Approach for providing constructive verbal feedback (Smith, Smoll, & Curtis, 1979), and principles of constructive feedback (Ginott, 1972).

PROVIDE ATHLETES WITH STRATEGIES TO PREPARE FOR AND COPE WITH FAILURE

Although coping with sport stress was briefly reviewed earlier, this chapter includes the ways in which sports coaches can assist athletes to properly cope with short-term and long-term sources of sport stress. The following strategies, not unlike any sport skills, have to be learned and practiced in order to be effective.

Have Reasonable Performance Expectations

As indicated earlier, failure is a perception. What is failure to one coach is a learning opportunity to another coach. Remind your players that (1) human performance is not consistently perfect. Flaws, errors, mistakes, and ultimately failing to meet expectations are inevitable. (2) Sport is a game; it is not life and death, so enjoy it. In addition to all-out effort, do not forget to make your sport experiences fun. And (3) your goal should be performance improvement, and giving 100% effort in your game preparation, training, and commitment to using performance outcomes as sources of growth and development.

Develop a Repertoire of Mental Skills

Describing the vast array of mental skills goes beyond the scope of this chapter. However, coaches should provide instruction on the best use of mental skills and the conditions under which each skill should be applied. Mental imagery (also called *visualization*), for instance, is best used before or between contests, and may distract the athlete from the task at hand during the contest. In games requiring high intensity it would be counterproductive to use relaxation techniques, which are more compatible with golf and other sports that require low exertion levels. Golfers and archers, for instance, should refrain from using a mental skill called *psyching up* and any other mental skills that raise the heart rate. *Anticipation* is a mental skill used in sports that include movement speed and rapid reaction time, such as basketball, soccer, and baseball hitting and fielding. Coaches will help athletes avoid failure by teaching the timing and proper use of mental skills.

Know When to Use Approach Coping

This book describes the use of two categories of coping with stress, approach and avoidance, each category with various types of specific coping techniques. Approach coping consists of physically or mentally thinking about or confronting the source of stress. *Effective* approach coping can entail asking the game official to explain his or her call, seeking information from the coach or a teammate, or reviewing and evaluating the condition under which the stressful situation occurred. *Ineffective* approach coping can include arguing, fighting, making intimidating statements, "trash talk," and negative self-talk (also called rumination, in which the athlete repeatedly recalls and mentally rehearses the stressful event).

When is approach coping most effective? Coping is a skill that requires time, so approach coping should be used only when there is sufficient time during the contest. Arguing the call, for instance, requires the athlete's attention and concentration; therefore, this is an inefficient coping technique when the ball is in play and the game is continuing. It is also best to avoid approach coping when the athlete is feeling anger or other negative emotions, which will, again, distract the athlete from the task at hand and may lead to a penalty—even expulsion from the contest.

Know When to Use Avoidance Coping

Avoidance coping consists of filtering out, reducing the importance of, or mentally distancing oneself from the source of stress. Avoidance coping is especially unique among elite athletes who are more capable than their less-skilled counterparts. This form of coping is particularly helpful when the game is in play and there is no time to deal with the stressful event. Specific avoidance coping strategies include psychological distancing (i.e., identifying the source of stress objectively), discounting (i.e., reducing the importance of the stressor), labeling (i.e., describing a person in a word or two that results in identifying selected characteristics such as "helpless" or "nasty"), and inattention (i.e., the ability to filter out unwanted or irrelevant sources of stress).

DESIRABLE DISPOSITIONS IN HANDLING FAILURE

Mental Toughness

Mental toughness in sports means reaching and sustaining high performance, particularly under pressure, by expanding capacity physically, mentally, and emotionally. Mentally tough athletes have the ability to ignore elements of interference during competition. Authors agree that mental toughness is learned, not inherited. One common, but false, view of many athletes and coaches is that we are born with the right "competitive instincts" and that not being able to handle failure is due to lacking the genetic predisposition to be mentally tough. The belief in a mental toughness gene is very tempting because it absolves the athlete of feeling responsible for performance failure. This is self-destructive thinking because the athlete is more likely to feel helpless, lack self-control about developing mental toughness, and lack the self-motivation to learn the proper mental skills to become more competitive.

Mentally tough competitors are self-motivated and self-directed; their energy comes from internal sources; it is not forced from the outside. Mentally tough athletes remain positive but realistic; they are builders and optimistic, not critics, fault finders, and pessimistic. They are in control of their emotions (they have "tamed the lion inside" in response to frustration and disappointment), calm and relaxed under fire (rather than avoiding pressure, they are challenged by it), highly energetic and ready for action (capable of getting themselves pumped up and energized for optimal effort and performance), determined (they have a strong will to succeed and are relentless in the pursuit of goals), mentally alert and focused (capable of long and intensive periods of full concentration), doggedly self-confident (have a high belief in their ability to perform well), and fully responsible (take full responsibility for their own actions).

Personal Traits of Mentally Tough Athletes

The literature reflects the following characteristics of mentally tough athletes. They have high self-esteem, have a sense of commitment, are self-disciplined, have a strong desire to succeed, feel personal accountability (responsible for performance outcomes), are competitive, have high but realistic self-expectations, have no (or controlled) fear of failure, have high goal orientation (very motivated by setting and meeting goals), and are hardy/resourceful.

Thoughts and Actions of Mentally Tough Athletes

Mentally tough athletes develop a pregame routine and have the ability to ignore elements of interference during competition. They also show emotional control, optimal arousal, confidence, intrinsic motivation, optimism, controlled anxiety, concentration and attentional control (alert and mentally focused), proper situational appraisals (challenge, not threat), good coping skills (deals effectively with adversity), and a sense of enjoyment in the competitive setting. These athletes perform automatically and project a positive attitude (positive body language),

Strategies for Building Mental Toughness

A review of literature shows the mentally tough athlete possesses these strategies for building mental toughness in sport, which, in turn, will improve the ability to overcome failure:

1. Maintains high (strength and endurance) fitness
2. Improves and uses mental skills
3. Sets realistic, but challenging, goals
4. Thinks positively and creates enthusiasm
5. Repeats self-positive affirmations (self-talk)
6. Maintains self-discipline (self-control)
7. Uses positive visualization (images successful/desirable performance)
8. Reviews film/video of best performances (or recalls them)
9. Prevents choking during contests, thinks about practice performance
10. Views competition as challenging, not threatening
11. Is confident in his or her ability and preparation
12. Thinks before (planning), not during, execution
13. Maintains external focusing on the task at hand
14. Ignores negative feelings and other distracting thoughts
15. Takes responsibility for own performance quality
16. Uses failure and coach feedback as motivators (sources of learning)
17. Attributes success to internal causes—high ability and effort
18. Dismisses thoughts of helplessness and hopelessness
19. Recalls successes, present and past
20. Thinks about positive role models
21. Maintains the need to learn

Coaches can create a mental toughness checklist for each athlete and, using a numerical scale, compare current scores with future scores, and build in strategies and interventions to improve the athlete's mental toughness total score.

Competitiveness

Naturally, all athletes want to win. However, athletes differ in their desire and motivation to win, a disposition called *win-orientation*. This orientation consists of three components: (1) competitiveness (the desire to strive for success in competition), (2) win orientation (focus on winning and avoid thoughts of losing), and (3) goal orientation (focus on creating and meeting personal goals). When completing an inventory that measures these dispositions, not surprisingly, athletes tend to score higher on all three, particularly competitiveness, and males score higher than females on all three dimensions. Researchers have found over the years that highly skilled athletes enjoy and optimally strive for success in competition, but tend to measure their success by performing at their personal best (performance goals) rather than by only winning or losing (outcome goals). The implication for coaches in reducing the negative effects of failure among athletes is that quality performance deserves at least as much recognition as the contest's outcome.

Sport Learned Resourcefulness

Learned resourcefulness (LR) is defined as having a repertoire of behavioral and cognitive skills that allows the athlete to regulate thoughts and emotions that might otherwise interfere with the athlete's goals and target behavior. LR strategies can help a person cope with discomfort, exertion, pain, or fatigue experienced during exercise (conditioning). LR may also help athletes maintain a weight control program, overcome feeling helpless, and prefer delayed gratification. LR strategies include positive self-talk, setting realistic but challenging goals, receiving and retaining strong social support, and reminders to conduct the proper mental skills at the appropriate time.

Sport Self-Control

A person with self-control voluntarily starts and maintains thoughts and behaviors under the proper environmental conditions that lead to reaching the athlete's short-term and long-term goals. An example of an effective strategy for self-control is to develop and carry out an action plan that includes behaviors to improve health, rehabilitation from injury, or sports performance. The result is long-term adherence to new health rituals. An action plan might include scheduling sleep and wake-up times, pre-sleep rituals for better rest, daily exercise, meals and snacks, planning sport skill practices, days and times to receive coaching, time needed to build new rituals, and obtaining social support. Self-control also includes having a plan B in case original plans are disrupted.

Confidence

Sport psychologists, coaches, and researchers agree that self-confidence is one of the most important mental states for success in sport competition. Self-confidence, also called sport confidence, is the athlete's belief about his or her ability to be successful in performing a desired skill. Sport self-confidence is typically defined as an athlete's belief that he or she can successfully execute a specific activity. It is not a personality trait and, therefore, does not describe the athlete's feelings beyond the sport environment or situation. Sport self-confidence is the athlete's belief or degree of certainty in a particular moment about his or her ability to be successful at sport. Highly confident athletes are more likely to have high self-expectations and to anticipate successful performance outcomes.

UNDESIRABLE DISPOSITIONS THAT CONTRIBUTE TO SPORT FAILURE

Depending on the situation, persistent failure in sport can have unpleasant consequences. Examples of undesirable dispositions include depression (acute and chronic), anxiety (short term and long term), and low future expectations. The purpose of this section is to describe dispositions that make the athlete increasingly susceptible to stress and perceived failure.

Depression

Depression is a mood disorder that ranges from mild to severe and, at more advanced stages, may reflect mental illness. Depression is usually depicted as a depressed mood or a loss of interest or pleasure in all or most activities for at least two consecutive weeks. Symptoms of depression include loss of appetite, weight loss or gain, disturbance of sleep, disruption of psychomotor skills, decreased energy, feeling worthless and guilty, poor concentration, and thoughts of suicide (Leith, 1998). Based on these symptoms, it is not surprising that depression strongly influences sport performance.

Leith's review of related literature indicates that exercising for 15 to 30 minutes at a time, particularly aerobic-type exercise, promotes mental health; therefore, that is also the time frame for improving symptoms of depression. More than 70 studies across a variety of age groups and both genders have shown that aerobic exercise reduces clinical (severe) depression.

Anxiety

Anxiety consists of feelings of threat or worry. It can either be acute (short term) or chronic (long term). Clinical anxiety is a form of mental illness that leads to changes in a person's thoughts and actions, occurs even without some initiating event, and leads to disproportionate and unmanageable responses. Anxiety is actually beneficial, even potentially lifesaving, under certain conditions (for instance, looking both ways before crossing the street, walking carefully on snow or ice, competing cautiously against the opposing sport team). However, in sport competition, excessive anxiety can also be debilitating to normal thinking, speed and accuracy of information processing, and sport performance. High acute (situational) anxiety, in both cognitive (e.g., feelings of worry or threat) and somatic (e.g., muscle tension) forms, is one of the strongest sources of mental distraction and poor performance in sport settings.

Aerobic (cardio) exercise markedly reduces both acute and chronic types of anxiety. This type of exercise include walking, jogging, running, swimming, cycling, and group aerobic classes. Exercise-induced changes in acute anxiety normally last two to four hours.

Self-Handicapping

As discussed in Chapter 1, sometimes athletes enter a contest with a self-defeating attitude. If they feel intimidated by their opponent, or feel their skills are not adequate to be victorious, they will compete with less effort, less enthusiasm, higher anxiety, and less concentration. Their attentional focus will be internal on negative feelings rather than external on the environment and on the actions of their opponent. This cascade of poor mental processes will result in slower processing of game-related information, greater muscular tension (which reduces motor coordination), and slower reaction time. The athletes who experience this condition will be unable to anticipate the actions of their opponent and, therefore, slow their own reactions to task demands. Collectively, the athlete's precontest pessimistic state of mind, which provides excuses for losing before performance outcomes are even known and justifies the anticipated lack of success, is called self-handicapping (Jones & Berglas, 1978). Self-handicappers do not link failure with their own low ability, thereby protecting their self-esteem. Losing is due, instead, to low motivation and poor effort.

Self-handicapping (SH) influences team cohesion if any individual member feels, before the contest, that he or she will not be at fault for group failure, yet takes full responsibility for group success. High social cohesion (i.e., the extent to which team members interacted positively away from the sport venue) is related to lower SH. In addition, low task cohesion (i.e., the degree of team harmony and effective interactions while executing performance skills during the game) is associated with high SH. Thus, SH enhances group cohesion because it improves members' sense of acceptance and support from others, increases the sharing of responsibility for team failure, and results in more acceptance by and support for other group members (Anshel, 2012).

Many coaches, however, like the idea of each team member feeling responsible for the performance and well-being of others (as in the old saying, "There is no *I* in *team*"). In addition, self-confidence and motivation are protected by individuals' propensity *not* to blame themselves following failure or poor performance. According to Carron, Hausenblas, and Eyrs (2005), use of SH strategies should be less necessary in highly cohesive groups. Responsibility for perceived failure is usually shared equally in cohesive groups, in which group support is readily available and there are fewer threats to self-esteem.

Social Loafing

Social loafing is a decrease in individual effort and performance due to the physical presence of other persons as opposed to performing the task alone

(Anshel, 1995; Hardy, 1990). Social loafing is evident only under conditions in which more than one person is performing the same task simultaneously. Examples include blocking by the offense in U.S. football, rowing, or group tackling in contact sports.

Usually social loafing occurs when athletes perceive the criterion (main) task as unimportant, meaningless, not intrinsically motivating, or being performed by relative strangers, especially (though not always) under noncompetitive conditions. Social loafing has been explained as a motivational loss, because individuals are less likely to feel accountable for the quality of their performance if they are held collectively responsible for task success. Social loafing may be strongly related to task duration; athletes may more likely loaf under conditions of fatigue, boredom, or prolonged repetition of the task (Anshel, 1995).

Karau and Williams (1993) concluded that social loafing occurs across many different types of tasks, including physical, cognitive, evaluative, and perceptual tasks. It is evident in both males and females and across different cultures. Karau and Williams concluded that the tendency to engage in social loafing increases when (1) the athlete's effort cannot be assessed independently of the group; (2) the athlete views the task as not meaningful; (3) the athlete views his or her contribution to the contest's outcome as redundant or irrelevant; (4) the athlete's personal involvement in the task is low; (5) the athlete questions the relevance of his or her contribution to the outcome; (6) the athlete's teammates are highly skilled and are expected to perform well; and (7) a comparison against group standards, that is, norms of high- versus low-quality performance, is not available.

Strategies for sport coaches for overcoming or preventing social loafing, according to Hardy (1990) and Karau and Williams (1993), include (1) identifying the athlete's efforts; (2) helping the athlete view his or her performance as making a unique and important contribution to the team's effort; (3) demonstrating that the task being performed is difficult but achievable; (4) having the athlete perform the task with teammates, as opposed to strangers, or as part of a group high in social cohesion; (5) ensuring that the task personally involves the athlete and that the athlete has a personal stake in the task's outcome; and (6) making each performer's task unique to increase a sense of control over their efforts and personal responsibility for performance outcomes.

Finally, one way to combat the mere perception of team social loafing is to build and maintain social support among team members. This entails having teammates interact and monitor each other's performance daily or regularly. Social support builds trust and helps minimize the likelihood of social loafing.

SELF-REGULATION

Self-regulation is typically defined as actions that occur when executing a task that allow performers to control or direct their activity through self-imposed rules or regulations. The goal of self-regulation is to adapt performance demands to varying circumstances, situations, or surroundings to minimize or prevent failure (Crews, Lochbaum, & Karoly, 2001).

To Zimmerman (1986), self-regulation consists of three subcomponents—metacognitive, motivational, and behavioral—each of which has implications for competitive sport. The *metacognitive* component consists of planning (e.g., What new rituals do I want to establish?), organizing (e.g., How can I set up practice conditions to learn and automate these new rituals?), self-instructing (e.g., How is my performance improving and what is needed to reach the next stage?), self-monitoring (e.g., fitness program and outcomes; skill development), and self-evaluating at various stages (e.g., level of competence and improvement). The *motivational* component consists of athletes who perceive themselves as competent, autonomous (independent), and confident. The *behavioral* component reflects selecting, structuring, and creating environments that optimize goal-directed behavior—that is, helping the athlete to achieve predetermined goals.

In competitive sport, for example, metacognitive self-regulation could include scheduling practice sessions for the day and week, preparing for practice and contests by bringing appropriate clothing for the anticipated session, ensuring availability of the facilities and proper equipment, requesting that the coach observe practice performance and provide insights into skill improvement, requesting input from a personal trainer, studying the playbook, observing others (e.g., teammates, opponents) perform the same skills directly or on videotape to serve as models for improving technique, and assessing performance quality.

In the motivational component, the athlete (and, perhaps, his or her coach) makes self-assessments that reflect competence (e.g., "I am performing the skills correctly" or "I need to improve on . . ."), the skills needed to complete each task independent of instruction, and confidence or self-efficacy (e.g., "I feel good and have met my performance goals").

An example of the *behavioral* component could be attending a rehabilitation session at a specific time and location, in the presence of a coach or therapist, using specific equipment, and obtaining instruction to achieve personal goals. Keeping attendance and performance records of therapeutic experiences and outcomes is also part of self-regulation.

Self-regulation in sport is based on the premise that the athlete is both self-motivated and capable of engaging independently in tasks that will lead to achieving goal-directed performance outcomes. If, for instance, we brush our teeth and floss regularly, we will be far less likely to suffer from dental and periodontal disease than if we did not perform these tasks. If an athlete engages in the proper training regimen and practices the requisite sport skills, performance success under competitive conditions is far more likely than if the practice of relevant skills and other game preparation are neglected. Self-regulation *failure* means that a person does not carry out the cognitive and behavioral strategies that are necessary for task success, and goals are not met. Although everyone self-regulates certain behavior patterns during their day, sometimes those behaviors are self-destructive and unhealthy. In sport, self-regulation is the athlete's attempt to ensure that desirable rituals are learned and carried out as planned.

ATHLETE EVALUATION PROCESS

The term *evaluation* is often associated with a negative, threatening, and unpleasant experience. Athletes view the process with mistrust and anxiety; the quality of their work is being criticized. When done correctly, however, the evaluation system is essential for helping athletes learn and grow. It is in this area where it is particularly important to acknowledge failure and to develop an action plan to build skills in addressing sources of failure.

Perhaps the final word on how effective leaders can—and should—promote failure among subordinates is from the well-known author of *Leadership: The Power of Emotional Intelligence*, Daniel Goleman (2011). Goleman explains that there are four capabilities of emotionally intelligent leaders. These are (1) self-awareness (recognizing not only one's own strengths but also one's weaknesses and working with group members who have superior skills in one's areas of weakness); (2) self-management (maintaining a balance and consistency of emotions, adapting to change, and being resilient in the face of adversity); (3) empathy (being a good listener to team members and taking the time to understand what they are saying and feeling); and (4) relationship skills (constantly inspiring and motivating team members and being aligned with the company's goals, yet at the same time managing conflict and maintaining a positive office environment).

High-quality leaders, including sports coaches, work with subordinates in ways that assure growth, skill development, opportunity, and confidence to achieve at the highest level possible for each individual. It would be accurate to conclude that good leaders do not give in to failure; they rise above it. They see promise while others see problems. They lead—relentlessly—because they are determined to one day reach and obtain their most important goals and performance outcomes. The high-quality leader is equally concerned with helping his or her subordinates, including athletes, reach their personal goals. Testimony to the use and encouragement of failure in the corporate world—and in sport—is the title of an article authored by former Procter & Gamble CEO, A. G. Lafley, on lessons learned the hard way, "I Think of My Failures as a Gift" (Dillon, 2011).

8

EFFECTIVE COMMUNICATION SKILLS FOR PERFORMANCE FEEDBACK AND INSTRUCTION

[People] who can learn from [their] own mistakes, will always be learning something.

—Evan Esar (1968, p. 467)

At the heart of *positive failure*—the central theme of this book—is effective communication. Sports coaches, athletes, or anyone else who possesses high-quality skills and performs at an elite level can have enormous talent. These skills are wasted, however, without the ability to communicate techniques that produce effective and consistent performance. This chapter addresses the type of communication skills that will help athletes (and other physical performers) to develop their skills and take necessary and intelligent risks toward learning and performance success. Coaching strategies to prevent and overcome failure are also included.

COACH COMMUNICATION SKILLS THAT ALLOW ATHLETES TO FAIL SAFELY

If failure is a perception, then acquiring that perception occurs through the coach's words and actions; in other words, coach communication. Many fine coaches are geniuses at planning team strategy, teaching performance techniques, and knowing the detailed rules of their sport. Sadly, however, many coaches are unable to effectively communicate their knowledge, due to the inability to establish an open and trusting relationship with players and/ or due to the lack of knowledge of proper teaching skills, a science called *sport pedagogy* or *educational sport psychology* (Anshel, 2012).

No one has more influence on and credibility in the player's thoughts, emotions, and behaviors than the team coach. This section addresses how this intense and meaningful relationship between coach and athlete can present the opportunity for athletes to feel secure in handling failure and learning how to fail safely and effectively. Here are some guidelines for effective communication to help athletes perceive the "benefits" of failing.

COACHING STRATEGIES TO PREVENT AND OVERCOME FAILURE

There are communication strategies that coaches can use that will provide athletes with enormous mental and emotional support, and create an atmosphere of mutual respect in making failure feedback positive, helpful, and nonthreatening. *Sport Psychology: From Theory to Practice* (Anshel, 2012) provides 14 guidelines for effective communication in sport psychology:

1. *Failure is good.* Remind the athletes that failure can be helpful and is expected in competitive sport. Tell them as a team while they gather together, and remind them confidentially and individually.

2. *Build your communication foundation.* Communication between coach and athlete is more effective if based on a foundation of mutual trust, honesty, sensitivity, and credibility. The foundation of communication tells that athlete not to take criticism personally, that the coach has a job to do in being judgmental, critical, even upset. Ginott (1972) reminds us that criticism is more effective when it reflects the person's behavior, not his or her character and personality. If an athlete agrees that the coach's criticism has value in helping the athlete improve in developing his or her skills, it won't be misunderstood and hurtful. "I trust my coach to provide assistance in helping to make me a better athlete" is a cornerstone of effective leadership and allows athletes to use critical feedback more effectively.

3. *Be honest.* Athletes want the truth about the coach's perceptions of their performance, otherwise they will not know what to do in order to improve and become better athletes. However, sometimes brutal honesty can do more harm than good. If you feel the athlete does not possess the requisite skills to be a high-quality competitor, keep that opinion to yourself and let the athlete advance as far as he or she can. No one can predict the future with absolute certainty.

4. *Do not be defensive.* If an athlete questions or disagrees with something, take a moment (if possible) to explain the instruction or issue. One coach replied to an athlete inquiry with, "Do it my way and don't ask any questions." That cut off a chance for the athlete to learn the purpose and value of the instruction, thereby making it more meaningful. Athletes need to feel secure in asking questions and asking for clarification, but yes, the coach makes the final decision on all matters unless otherwise stated.

5. *Be consistent with your communication style and your relationship with your players.* Being friendly and supportive one day, then unfriendly and cold the next day is confusing to others and reduces confidence in developing trust between the coach and athlete.

6. *Show empathy toward each player.* Being a competitive athlete, especially at the elite level, is filled with considerable pressure to succeed; to endure close and regular judgment by teammates, coaches, and spectators; to make a "good" impression on others; to compete with pain and discomfort; and to outplay opponents (and selected teammates for more play time). The demands and expectations to perform flawlessly are immense. Therefore, coaches should be part of the solution, not part of the problem, helping athletes deal with these demands, especially when dealing with the inevitable experiences of failure. After an athlete makes an error, a coach should tell him or her, "Keep trying; do not give up. Think about what you learned from the error and how you can correct it."

7. *Never use sarcasm.* Failure can be an ugly experience if comments and instructional feedback contain sarcasm (e.g., "Even my mother can shoot the ball better than that," or "Nice play, rubber hands"). Sarcasm is used to humiliate the player and destroys player loyalty toward his or her coach.

8. *Praise and criticize behavior, not personality.* Praise and criticism are inherent components of instructional feedback, providing approval, and

raising the athlete's confidence. It is imperative, however, that both types of feedback be constructive and promote learning, especially after failure. The late psychiatrist Dr. Haim Ginott (1969) would recommend praising and criticizing behavior, not character or personality. Praising behavior sounds like "Great that you stayed with your opponent on that play, Betty." Praising character, conversely, would be "You are great." Criticizing behavior would be, "Mike, you need to get into position quickly when we call X play." Criticizing character would be, sadly, "Are you deaf? How many times do I have to tell you to keep your hands up when guarding the basket?"

The correct use of praise has been demonstrated in a model by Smith, Smoll, and Curtis (1979). Their "sandwich approach" is a model for offering praise while teaching skills and is especially effective when providing instructional feedback after an error. The underlying philosophy of this approach is to ignore the past mistake—or at least not to overemphasize it—and, instead, focus on future performance.

9. *Respect the integrity of others.* Integrity is roughly defined as demonstrating honesty and sincerity. It is similar to character in that a person with integrity has moral strength, reputation, and status. Coaches who fail to recognize their athletes' integrity are showing a lack of respect toward the performers' individuality, ability, and "humanness"—their unique qualities that contribute to the team. Arrogance toward others is an example of no integrity and informs athletes that failure is not to be tolerated. Instead, it warrants punishment.

10. *Use positive nonverbal cues.* Thumbs up, a pat on the back, and a smile are examples of nonverbal praise. These signs reflect the coach's approval and recognition toward the athlete and are interpreted as favorable; nonverbal praise has strong motivational value because these signs recognize skill improvement (often, following earlier failure).

11. *Interact consistently with all team members.* Yes, each sports team has starters and nonstarters. But does that mean nonstarters are less important or should be treated differently than their starting teammates? Coaches who allow starters to use a different set of team rules than their nonstarting teammates are compromising team cohesion and player loyalty. It's disrespectful and condescending toward the nonstarting players and creates a double standard for team behavior. Everyone warrants attention, instruction, respect, tolerance, and approval.

12. *Do not confuse arrogance with confidence.* Athletes must be confident in performing their skills at the highest level with some degree of consistency. It is one of the most important mind-sets an athlete can have—and must have. Confidence is typically defined as an internal thought process, that is, the athlete's belief about his or her ability to successfully perform a desired skill (Feltz, 1988). Highly confident athletes are more likely to have high self-expectations and to anticipate successful performance outcomes. Confidence is not the same as arrogance, however.

Some people confuse the concepts and definitions of confidence with arrogance. To begin this comparison, confidence is a feeling; an internal state. Arrogance is reflected by action or behavior. The dictionary defines arrogance as "full of or due to pride; to claim or seize without right" (*Webster's New World Dictionary*, 1984, p. 34). A person demonstrates arrogance by appearing to show—by actions or words—his or her superiority. Examples can be behavioral (e.g., ignoring you even though you know each other) or verbal (e.g., making critical statements that infer the person possesses superior characteristics; expressing criticism; making unfavorable comparisons such as "our team is so much better than yours"). What is clear about arrogant people is that they are usually covering up aspects of their personality or self-esteem, revealing deep-rooted insecurity and an overcompensation for having lower skills and less confidence than others. Arrogance is often a facade. The important point to remember is that coaches should promote confidence in their players and not confuse confidence with arrogance; one is very necessary to succeed in sport and to handle failure, while the other one is unnecessary and impedes growth, development, and performance success. One of the most confident professional athletes in major league baseball was Don Drysdale, pitcher for the Los Angeles Dodgers (see page 102).

13. *The sandwich approach.* This technique, developed by sport psychology professors Smith, Smoll, and Curtis (1979) and still used widely today, offers constructive feedback to athletes in a sensitive, yet effective, manner. It is called a "sandwich" because two positive statements are sandwiched around a feedback statement about proper future performance. This technique consists of three elements that are verbalized in the following sequence: (1) a positive statement, (2) future-oriented positive feedback, and (3) a compliment. Here is an example of applying the sandwich approach:

Positive statement: "Good job of looking the ball into your hands, Janice."
Future-oriented feedback: "On that next grounder come forward and stay on your toes, not your heels."
Compliment: "You're improving nicely, Janice. Keep practicing."

Smith et al.'s (1979) sandwich approach provides younger (youth sport) athletes with positive and constructive messages following errors and other forms of performance failure. In the parlance of child clinical psychologist Dr. Haim Ginott (1965), this feedback style "preserves the child's self-respect" and "statements of understanding precede statements of advice or instruction" (p. 25). The coach's sensitive and empathetic response to the young athlete's error "serves as an emotional Band-Aid for the child's bruised ego" (p. 24). Ginott's key concept is *empathy*. He contends that "we so phrase our words that the child knows we understand what he has gone through" (p. 27). The sandwich approach embodies one additional concept from Ginott: reflecting behavior, not character or personality, in the content of our feedback. In Ginott's words, "Only conduct can be condemned or commended, feelings cannot and should not be" (p. 39). This communication would be beneficial not only to children, but to people of all ages.

14. *Never combine anger with instruction.* Psychologists agree that we—all of us, children and adults of all ages, athletes and coaches, supervi-

---

The late Don Drysdale, major league all-star pitcher from the 1960s, confirmed that his success was clearly linked to his confidence level, although some might mistake his thinking as arrogance, not confidence. Remember, however, that arrogance can be observed, while confidence is a thought or emotion—or both. Drysdale's record was 209 wins and 166 losses, with a highly respectable earned run average of 2.95; he was a member of eight National League all-star teams. According to the Official Site of Don Drysdale, he once said, "I hate all hitters. I start a game mad and I stay that way until it's over" ("About Don Drysdale," n.d.). If an opposing pitcher knocked down (i.e., pitched inside) or hit one of his teammates, Drysdale would double the retaliation by knocking down or hitting two of his opponents. That's a sign of extreme mental toughness. Don Drysdale was mediocre in his early years but quickly became one of baseball's most competitive and successful pitchers.

---

sors and subordinates—are entitled to our feelings. Based on the nature of relationships between two or more individuals (e.g., coach versus athlete; child versus parent or teacher), there are limits to how our feelings should be conveyed. However, the words "I feel . . ." should always be allowed if the message is meant to share feelings rather than to humiliate, upset, or threaten another person, at least in healthy relationships (Ginott, 1965, 1972). As Ginott contends, "Anger, like a hurricane, is a fact of life to be acknowledged and prepared for" (1965, p. 56). "We want to get our point across and let the stormy clouds evaporate" (p. 57).

Ginott's (1965, pp. 57–58) model for managing anger within the context of competitive sport begins with "three truths." First, "we accept the fact that (athletes/subordinates) will make us angry." Second, "we are entitled to our angry feelings without guilt or shame." Third, "we can express our angry feelings provided we do not attack the (athlete's/subordinate's) personality or character" (e.g., "You asked a real stupid question;" "That was a foolish thing to do"). *Sarcasm* is another communication killer, especially when mixed with anger (e.g., "What are you, deaf? Didn't I already tell the team what we need to do to score?").

Ginott (1965) suggests that handling "turbulent feelings" begins by labeling those feelings aloud (e.g., "I feel irritated when you drop the ball due to a lack of concentration" or "I am upset that you refuse to go all-out in practice"). The second step is to express the reason(s) for our anger (e.g., "You are not training very hard, Bill. How do you expect to overcome your opponent when he will have more energy and perseverance late in the game? When I see you going at half speed I get upset and don't think you really want to play this game"). Finally, express what behavior needs to change (e.g., "Sue, when the ball is in play I expect you to field your position and give 100% effort. It's one thing if your opponent outplays you, but it is entirely another thing if you refuse to give full effort and perform the skills you have; you are better than that.").

Why is anger so damaging to learning? Why should coaches never provide instruction when they are angry? Primarily because expressing anger toward the athlete (or anyone else) creates a substantial rise in the receiver's anxiety level. Anxiety is a feeling of worry or threat. It is natural to feel threatened when verbally attacked by an angry coach (or boss). A sudden increase in anxiety directly interferes with the processing of information that includes storing verbal messages into memory. Because the athlete is so consumed by the coach's anger, the message content is ignored. What should the coach do? Express anger first (not insulting or humiliating the athlete) followed by a deep breath and a few seconds; then deliver the information feedback. It might sound like this: "Jill, I am upset that you forgot to take your position on defense, allowing the other team to score. We practiced that play many times, and you performed it in practice just fine. Next time I want you to concentrate and carry out that defensive play at 100% effort, is that understood?" Incidentally, critical feedback is always better remembered if the athlete is not criticized in front of the team; that is another anxiety raiser. Try to provide feedback as privately and confidentially as possible. Following these guidelines will allow failure to be experienced with far less pain and anguish.

INSTRUCTION AND COMMUNICATION
IN PROFESSIONAL (ELITE LEVEL) SPORT

In 1990, George F. Will authored a book called *Men at Work: The Craft of Baseball*. He presented the game of baseball as far more complex and sophisticated than sports fans can imagine. Failure plays a prominent role in Will's book. For instance, according to Will, "former baseball manager and current Hall of Famer Tony La Russa believes in taking risks precisely because baseball, the game of failure, is all risks, the odds being what they are against" (p. 39).

Risk Taking

The only way to experience positive failure is to take reasonable risks. Clearly, some people more than others are more likely to risk losing, making a mistake, experiencing failure, even being injured. Risk taking is a disposition; it's a part of one's personality. According to Malone's (1985) review of literature in this area, athletes tend to be greater risk takers than their nonathlete peers. The athlete's perception of danger creates excitement and a desire to master the environment and the skills needed to succeed. Still, skilled (elite) performers will not take unnecessary risks in tasks and conditions for which they are not prepared and trained.

Why are elite athletes more likely than nonathletes to take risks that could lead to failure? The answer might be due to certain personality characteristics. Elite athletes tend to score higher for stimulus seeking; optimal arousal; competitiveness; confidence; what has been called facilitative anxiety, which reflects an athlete's perception that her anxiety (feelings of worry or threat) will benefit, rather than inhibit, her performance, not unlike the need to look both ways before crossing the street (Jones, Hanton, & Swain, 1994); heightened (cognitive and somatic) arousal; and better performance in the presence of an audience than when performing alone with no audience present. The question remains, however, whether many athletes are unable to achieve at the highest level and meet their performance potential due to excessive anxiety that leads to fear of failure and that is too high and uncontrollable.

Risk taking is directly linked failure in these ways: (1) the extent to which athletes perceive risk taking as tied to performance failure; (2) the level of risk involved, or conversely, the probability of success; (3) the level of fear about the consequences of failure; and (4) the level of value placed on achieving a predetermined outcome—the goal. As Maxwell (2000) says, "Risk must be evaluated not by the fear it generates in you or the probability of your success, but by the value of the goal" (p. 144). "To achieve any worthy goal, you must take risks" (Maxwell, 2000, p. 146).

Inches Separate Performance Success and Failure

The culture of sports competition, the people who coach the game, and those who play it are so quick to categorize performance outcomes as good, bad, winning, and losing. Sport success is about the end product; winning, losing, number of hits, points, tackles, goals, speed (i.e., performance time), and accuracy (i.e., percentage of desirable outcomes versus attempts). What is forgotten in this rush to judgment when one opponent is publically designated as the winner and the other opponent is categorized as the loser is the closeness with which both competitors perform to exchange outcomes. This same process separates individuals who compete professionally (or go to the Olympic Games) in contrast to those whose performance is deserving of success—even stardom—but fall below the winners by a matter of inches, seconds, or milliseconds (thousandths of a second). This is partly the reason it is so sad to label performance based primarily on outcome as opposed to the quality of skill execution that occurred during the contest. Failure and success are fleeting. A baseball player is judged favorably if he or she gets a hit only 3 out of 10 times, resulting in a batting average of .300. Very few sports and conditions allow such mediocrity—3 out of 10—to be acceptable.

In his very complete analysis of the game of professional baseball, Will (1990) reports that "the difference between the major and minor leagues is just a matter of inches and consistency. This is essentially true of the difference between excellence and mere adequacy in poetry or surgery or anything else" (p. 326).

Perhaps the answer is to examine success and failure based on the on-going processes that are performed during the contest. Examples include hitting the ball hard despite making an out, the number of successful passes in basketball, or the number of shots taken in ice hockey or kicks in soccer that reach the opponent's goal but are blocked. Will calls baseball "a game especially unforgiving of minor mistakes" (1990, p. 328). That's an understatement when you consider the required reaction speed in response to a 90-mile-per-hour pitched baseball:

> A 90-mile-per-hour fastball that leaves a pitcher's hand 55 feet from the plate is traveling 132 feet per second and will reach the plate in .4167 second. . . . Having decided to try to hit the pitch, the batter has about two-tenths of a second to make his body do it. The ball can be touched by the bat in about 2 feet of the pitch's path, or for about 15-thousandths of a second [15 milliseconds]. So anyone who hits a ball thrown by a major league pitcher—even just puts the ball in play—is doing something remarkable. The consistently good hitters are astonishing. (pp. 192–193).

Perhaps not surprisingly, Will (1990) contends that "the different degrees of superiority in terms of natural physical skills are less marked and less important than another difference. It is the difference in the intensity of the application to the craftsmanship of baseball. Some people work harder than others, a lot harder" (p. 327). This is commonly referred to as "playing hard." As Will explains, baseball is such a humbling game. "The exultation of success is going to be followed in short order by the cold slap of failure. . . . So why get high when a low is just around the corner?" (p. 141). Thus, it is important to know the proper reactions to failure, since failure is inherent in sport.

9

FAILURE AND CHILDREN
Helping Kids Fail Safely

We are programmed at an early age to think that failure is bad.
That belief prevents (children) and organizations from effectively
learning from their missteps.

—Tavis Smiley (2011, p. 3)

Playing sport, either for recreation or as part of skilled competition, is a part of childhood experiences in most cultures. Participating in sport, however, is becoming increasingly important in contemporary society because children are becoming less and less physically active. As a result, children are becoming obese and unhealthy, and it's continuing into adulthood. Sport participation is one way to encourage children to develop habits that encourage physical activity and maintain a healthier lifestyle. Physical activity, in general, and sport participation, in particular, are necessary components of growth and development. One structure that encourages physical activity among children (and adolescents) is youth sports (i.e., sports competition under the age of 14 years; Anshel, 2012).

While organized sport offers a vast array of opportunities to learn new sport skills, be physically active, make new friends, learn to deal with adversity under competitive conditions, and just have fun, participating in sports competition can also be highly unpleasant, stressful, and physically harmful. While a review of the youth sports literature related to dropping out goes beyond the scope of this chapter, it is apparent that a child's inability to deal with failure is a major component in the dropout problem.

A CHILD ATHLETE'S FAILURE TO DEAL WITH FAILURE

Among the main reasons for participating in youth sport are having fun, learning new skills, and meeting new friends. Sadly, children are dropping out of youth sport in very large numbers. The dropout rate from organized youth sport in most Western countries often exceeds 70% (Anshel, 2012). Perhaps not surprisingly, the reasons for dropping out mirror the reasons for participating—lack of fun, too many errors, poor sport skills, and lack of social support (e.g., no friendships with peers, excessive parental expectations, parental and coach criticism). Child athletes are especially vulnerable to experiencing failure more frequently and more intensely than their adult counterparts. Let's review some of the more apparent reasons children drop out of sport and what can be done to reduce—or even prevent—it by creating less harmful responses to failure.

PERCEIVED LACK OF ABILITY AND COMPETENCE

Most of us do not maintain participation in any area in which we do not feel successful. If computer programming is not performed at a high level we avoid this type of activity, or soon quit after experiencing failure. We rarely engage in activities we do not enjoy and feel competent at performing. Children are the same way. If child athletes feel they lack the proper level of skill and do not possess the ability to be successful in competitive sport, they will quit. Not surprisingly, the demonstrated lack of sport skill combined with critical information feedback (communicated primarily by adults—the child's coach and/or parents) further reinforces these thoughts and decisions.

Children have concluded they are failures in the athletic domain—"I'm not a good athlete"—rather than concluding they have failed on a specific task or condition (e.g., "I have a hard time catching the ball when the ball is thrown more than 10 yards"). This is especially sad, given that the main reason children play sports is to have fun and learn skills. Somewhere along the way their perceived competence significantly decreased and sport became no longer enjoyable.

Who gave child athletes, who just wanted to have fun through sport participation, messages they were not good enough and they lacked the skill to be successful? From what source did child athletes conclude they were not good enough to play and enjoy sports? Perhaps even more important for this book, who took the time to teach child athletes how to handle mistakes, errors, and failure when trying to perform very difficult and complex sport skills? What adults can do about helping children deal with perceived failure is described later in this chapter.

LOW INTRINSIC MOTIVATION/LACK OF ENJOYMENT

While intrinsic motivation (IM) was described earlier, it is important to note that IM plays an important part of a child's decision to enter and continue his or her participation in youth sports. The lack of IM is an important reason in the child's decision to drop out. Briefly, IM reflects a person's need to engage in an activity for fun, enjoyment, and satisfaction. A person's feelings of enjoyment, fun, and satisfaction when participating in an activity increase when he or she feels a sense of competence in that activity. It's called *perceived competence*: individuals view their level of performance positively; they consider themselves competent. This means (1) they have been given instruction on performing sport skills correctly, (2) they note improvement in their performance over time, and (3) they are given positive constructive information feedback on their performance by a credible source such as a coach or parent. However, this does not mean that the child athlete has been taught how to handle or react to the perception of failure and not meeting performance expectations. IM is further reduced when the level of sport skills of child athletes are compared unfavorably against each other.

BETWEEN-CHILD COMPARISONS

Often children determine their skill level in sport by comparing themselves on an array of motor/sport skills with others their age. This process is called *comparative appraisal*. Because children have relatively little past experience in sport against which to compare their skills, a process called self-appraisals, they depend on coaches, parents, teammates, and spectators to provide them with performance feedback. Sometimes the comparison process is based on external observations.

Young athletes are provided with many external sources of performance feedback in the appraisal process. Providing child athletes with feelings of success is the overall objective. This input comes in verbal and nonverbal forms, both positive and negative. Positive appraisals include verbal statements that reflect recognition and praise, while negative verbal appraisal includes reprimands and rejection, both of which can lead to self-appraisals of inadequacy, low ability, stress, and feelings of not belonging on the team. If these perceptions are not balanced by more positive thoughts, quitting the sport often results.

After determining the sources of feedback, it is the responsibility of adults to help prevent children from making appraisals that are inaccurate and inappropriate—remember, these are *children*, not miniature adults, performing complex motor skills with relatively little instruction and opportunities for practice. For instance, children can pick up the nonverbal signals of their coach and parents, who can telegraph pride and approval on the positive side, or embarrassment, annoyance, and disappointment on the negative side. Body language (e.g., facial expressions, eye contact, ignoring the youngster) is a powerful messenger that affects the child athlete's confidence, mood state, level of enjoyment, and an appraisal of his or her skills—success or failure.

Adult sport leaders—coaches and administrators—and parents need to collectively help each child athlete improve his or her sport skills and compare current with previous performance quality, called *intra-individual comparisons*. This way, the child athlete's improvement over time can be noted, resulting in far more likelihood of remaining a sports competitor and not dropping out. Less desirable is to compare children against each other. Unfavorable comparisons are likely to lead to less enjoyment, reduced confidence, and other undesirable characteristics. Every child has his or her own strengths and weaknesses. Statements such as "If Jon can do it, why can't you?" are very destructive and may lead young athletes to conclude they are not good enough to belong on the team. Being different does not necessarily mean the other player is better. Comparison appraisals are useful if combined with within-athlete (improvement over time) appraisals; however, informing child athletes that they lack the skills of others and that this will prevent them from competing is a message of rejection—"You are not good enough." Make sure child athletes have the opportunity to practice, receive instruction, and detect progress in their skills.

HANDLING FAILURE AMONG CHILD ATHLETES

How do we make child athletes handle and tolerate failure, learning from mistakes without being discouraged and eventually quitting the activity? There are guidelines and specific ways for adults (e.g., sports coaches, parents, teachers, sports administrators, sports officials) to help children deal constructively with failure.

Set Up Realistic Expectations

Why do adults expect perfect performance and skill mastery from young athletes who have not physically matured or been given the time, instruction, proper equipment, and sufficient practice needed for success in sport? An 8-year-old allows a hit baseball to go through his or her legs, and we call that an error. Fine, so what can the youngster learn from that mistake? How can coaches and parents provide the child with instruction and opportunities for more practice? Why demonize, harshly criticize, and reprimand the youngster? Why do we expect the same level of competence from child athletes that we expect from professionals? What is wrong with this picture? Adults need to have and show expectations of player behavior that are realistic and kind. They are children, not miniature adults. We do not want our children quitting opportunities to play sports. It may be their only chance to be physically active during the week and to transfer those sport skills through their life in recreational settings.

Develop Positive Relationships Between Child Athletes and Their Coach

Child athletes are less afraid to fail if they trust that their coach will teach skills by providing information feedback. They depend on their coach to help them mature and grow as sports competitors. Feedback can be given without anger, threats, sarcasm, and punishment. Guidelines for providing critical feedback to children are provided by the late child psychiatrist Dr. Haim Ginott (1965, 1969).

Ways to develop positive relationships between coach and players include the following: use the players' first names for all communication content, point out specific actions that need improvement (e.g., "Watch the ball into your glove, Jane"), avoid criticizing the player's character (e.g., "That was a stupid play, Jack"), do not reprimand the child athlete, avoid humiliation (i.e., making comments that embarrass the child, especially in front of peers and observers), and avoid sarcasm at all costs—it betrays the child's trust and respect in the coach. In addition, try to give each player skill instruction during the week or before the contest, and help each one apply those skills during the contest. Good coaches are good teachers. Therefore, skill instruction is essential for improvement and heightens perceived competence. Note, specifically, the areas of each athlete's performance that have improved.

Give Children Opportunities to Learn, Practice (With Verbal and Visual Feedback), and Compete

How often do child athletes receive skill instruction, especially with feedback on their performance? How often do we see child athletes sitting on the bench and being given no opportunity to compete? Coaches need to provide opportunities for their child athletes to practice and to learn sports skills. Child athletes should not be "thrown into" competitive games without preparation, practice, skill development, and to some degree skill mastery. And child athletes should be taught about ways to anticipate and respond properly to errors, mistakes, and failure, all of which are inevitable.

Practice Game Simulation

The key word in preparing athletes for competing in contests is *simulation*. *Game simulation* means that practice partly consists of performing sport skills under game-like conditions, then taking those experiences directly into the actual competition. Negative forms of perceived failure occur when children are asked to perform sport skills in the contest without proper preparation and practice. And this feeling of failure is what leads to dropping out.

Do Not Predict a Child's Future

Why do some adults—coaches and parents of child athletes, in this case—have a need to "play God" and predict a young athlete's future in sport? Does it give adults more power and influence over a child's life when they can say, with some certainly (they think), that "Kathy does not have the arm/ speed/ motivation/mental toughness [fill in the blank] to play shortstop." Given limited opportunities to learn and practice, and the relatively few experiences to compete in sport, do we really know the capability of any child athlete? Are we really in a position to dictate to children in which sport and even position they should compete?

A review of the talent identification literature suggests that the ability to predict a child's future sport success is very low (Anshel & Lidor, 2012). There are too many factors that go into improved sports performance to allow one person to predict a young athlete's future. This includes opportunities for practice and instruction, availability of high-quality coaching, close proximity of sports facilities, owning proper equipment, growth and maturation of the individual athlete, peer group and parental acceptance of sports involvement, and how athletes deal with failure. Each of these factors influences the child's future in sport. Somewhat on the fringe of these factors are the athlete's personality and genetic predisposition, none of which is controllable.

Coaches and parents need to stop predicting the child athlete's future success in a given sport and allow the young player to learn, develop, and mature at his or her own pace—with proper coaching—in order to reach his or her full potential. We simply do not know enough about the psychological factors that predict future success in sport. The act of predicting an athlete's future—referred to as "playing God" because the predictor claims to have the power to anticipate a young athlete's future—is very demotivating. Athletes—and their coaches—should feel that sport success comes from practice and instruction. The athlete is shortchanged in his or her wish to excel and achieve at the highest level—all because a few adults are certain about the young athlete's potential. For believers in a higher power, there is only one source of certainty about the future, and coaches (parents) are not that source.

Provide Performance Feedback Both During and After Contests

"Positive failure" is about learning from mistakes—without embarrassing the competitor. Competitive athletes in youth sport settings are in 100% agreement that coaches who verbally abuse athletes, particularly in the presence of teammates, lose the loyalty of their athletes (Anshel, 2012). While feedback during and after the contest is often advantageous to the athlete's development, performance feedback during and after contests should be subdued, conducted in private and not in the presence of others (unless similar feedback content reflects more than one performer), be specific and performance based, never attempt to insult the athlete's character, and consist of not more than one or two items (even if the coach has a "laundry list" of criticisms). Most people of all ages, including athletes, cannot process and reflect on more than two critical feedback issues at one time. More than two issues is overwhelming and communicates the impression and perception of overall incompetence.

Talk to the Child Athletes' Parents

The relationship between the child's coach and parents should always remain positive, open, and continuous. This is not to say that coaches should be held accountable to the child's parents; however, not unlike a school teacher informing parents of their child's school grades and areas of the student's strengths and areas of future growth, the coach should have an open dialogue with parents during the season about (1) their child's current status, (2) their child's areas of competence and in what areas future improvement is needed, and (3) the development of an action plan to improve the athlete's competence and ensure the young athlete will have an opportunity to compete. When adults team up to help the child succeed it's called *failing safely*.

Teach Sports Skills

Good coaches are good teachers. Without high-quality instruction, performance does not improve; it's as simple as that. The science of teaching sport skills is called *sports pedagogy*, so there is a science to good teaching. The best coaches do not always have the best players, but they are superior teachers and can communicate skills and strategies very effectively so that players can actually learn, improve, and apply their knowledge.

Teach Mental Skills

Sport, as well as other forms of physical performance, requires the use of physical skills to become successful. However, the athlete who has control of a set of mental skills (coping, visualization, how to perceive failure/errors) is more likely to win—to play consistently at a superior level—than competitors who ignore mental skills. Each mental skill has a specific technique and is optimally effective when used under certain circumstances. These skills serve the purposes of improving concentration, reducing (or managing) stress and anxiety, improving attentional focusing, increasing sport and exercise performance, and building confidence, among many other desirable outcomes. An array of books on "the mental game" is available in libraries, bookstores, and, of course, online.

Do Not Teach When Angry

When adults—sports coaches and parents of athletes—express anger toward a child athlete, two principles should be kept in mind at all times (see Ginott, 1965, 1969, for guidelines for providing useful instruction and the use of anger). First, express emotions and feelings that reflect frustration and anger *before not during* instructional feedback. Coach or parent anger results in two reactions from most athletes: (1) filtering out all content of the angry message and (2) experiencing anxiety. Therefore, any instruction that is expressed while the adult is upset tends to be filtered out. It is not integrated as useful instruction, and the value of using failed performance as a learning tool is lost.

The second principle is that adults who verbally express anger should never attack the child athlete's character or personality. Rather, address the child athlete's action or inaction—something tangible and observable to all parties. Ginott (1965) calls for using constructive, not destructive, criticism. "Constructive criticism confines itself to pointing out how to do what has to be done, entirely omitting negative remarks about the personality of the child" (p. 51). Avoid reacting to child misbehavior with insults and sarcasm that result in humiliation and embarrassment. Instead, identify with the child's own feelings of making an error (e.g., "That was a difficult play and I know you are disappointed, but let's keep practicing and work hard to improve"). Ginott suggests that as adults, we "can express . . . angry feelings provided we do not attack the child's personality or character" (p. 58).

Remember to Help Kids Have Fun

Since this is the primary reason children play sports, it is important to follow this guideline. "Lack of fun" and stress are the main reasons children drop out of sports programs. Shameful! It is not suggested that winning is unimportant and that child athletes with poor skills should be required to play in every game—and fail. What is suggested is that we provide effective, often individualized, sport skill instruction to child athletes and integrate them into competitive conditions—even if exclusively in practice games so they can perform and practice their skills under game conditions. Children need to learn ways to deal properly with the demands of competition without feeling berated and humiliated. "Never punish child athletes for making errors" should be etched in stone. Punishing children by requiring them to exercise to excess (e.g., running laps, sprints, push-ups) should be banned by school systems, not just with specific programs and courses. We need to expect performance errors from children and not react with deep disappointment and anger.

According to a position statement by the National Association for Sport and Physical Education (NASPE, 2009), "Administering or withholding physical activity as a form of punishment and/or behavior management is an inappropriate practice" and "coaches should never use physical activity or peer pressure as a means of disciplining athlete behavior" (p. 17). Exercise when used for disciplinary purposes, they claim, is a form of corporal punishment and is illegal in 29 states.

SHOULD EVERY YOUTH SPORTS COMPETITOR RECEIVE A TROPHY?

Trophies have been an inherent part of being a youth sport participant for many years. Usually, trophies have been allocated to those athletes who have earned them through some form of achievement and consistent, high-quality performance (e.g., most valuable . . . , best . . .). Traditionally, not everyone on the team would receive, nor "deserve," a trophy or other award due to the within-team competitive nature of the trophy recognizing "the best." This selective approach to awards led, in part, to a high dropout rate among youth sport participants; studies suggest a dropout rate of about 70% to 72% of athletes under the age of 14 years. The response, called an "overreaction" by some traditionalists and the athletes' parents, was to ensure that all participants received a trophy or some other type of award in recognition of their participation (Murphy, 1999). These individuals want to eliminate a young athlete's sense of failure from sports competition so they remain engaged and do not quit sport. But now there seems to be a very strong negative reaction to that policy, which was determined and policed at a local (not national) level.

Apparently, some parents are fighting back against the trophy-for-everybody policy. The national media (Brady, 2015, p. 7C) recently reported a story concerning a parent's decision to return the trophies his two sons obtained from their youth sports league based on their mere participation rather than having achieved a high standard of performance. The actions were that of a National Football League player from the Pittsburgh Steelers, linebacker James Harrison. According to the story, "he was taking away participation trophies awarded to his sons, ages 8 and 6, until they 'EARN a real trophy'" (p. 7C). Harrison's explanation was that he was "not about to raise two boys to be men by making them believe they are entitled to something just because they tried their best" (p. 7C).

Not surprisingly, the executive director of the Awards and Personalization Association, Ms. Louise Ristau, said, "Recently it's been rather trendy to be negative toward participation awards and to blame them for kids feeling entitled or not learning to be competitive. . . . But what's really causing that? It is really a participation award or the environment they're living in?" (p. 7C).

So what is the answer? The CEO of an industry that makes trophies, Mr. Scott Sletten, said he questions the point of giving participation trophies to older athletes (e.g., adolescent ages), "but with these younger kids, who most of these things are for, it's just encouraging participation" (p. 7C). Sletten contends that it's a good thing to recognize child athletes for performing competently and they "did something good" (p. 7C). Can the two sides of this argument be negotiated and a compromise reached in which some form of award is distributed without minimizing its importance and the message of competence it is supposed to convey?

Here are two ideas about distributing awards to youth sport athletes that seem reasonable and will have a motivational effect on the athlete to value the award and to reflect competence in sport. After all, we want children and adolescents to play sports over their lifetime, if possible. Physical activity is desirable and badly needed for persons of *all* ages. We want to have our kids develop healthy habits and attitudes toward activity starting early in life. Sport is one common and enjoyable vehicle to experience an active lifestyle, control weight, and have better health.

Everyone receives a trophy—but . . . The first idea follows IM theory (see Anshel, 2012, for a description), that is, how to provide a trophy for every team member that recognizes something he or she did that reflected competent performance from the preceding season. IM theory indicates that motivation to maintain participation in an activity is to feel competent in performing the activity. The issue is to be sure that the reason for the trophy is indicated and understood by the performer. So, there can be two most valuable players, or everyone who made the league's all-star team, or fastest runner, or most successful pinch hitter (or substitute); there can also be a reward for team statistician, the most improved player, or the best (most successful) base stealer. The list goes on until each and every team member is recognized for something that showed his or her competence or improvement. The award has meaning and is not trivialized.

Trophies versus certificates. The second idea concerns developing different categories of recognition. Why not have primary awards and secondary awards that recognize different types and levels and competencies of sport involvement. Primary awards—trophies—should reflect performance competence, as was originally intended. This should include being a member of the championship (or division) team. There is no reason why every member of the championship team should not deserve a trophy. Of course each member contributed to the final outcome—even showing up regularly for practice and games but not starting. Certificates, on the other hand, should be allocated to every member of the league or program. The certificate can recognize participation, perhaps using the words "performed successfully," "performed competently during the season," "achieved personal performance goals," "showed good improvement during the season," "demonstrated good improvement in skilled performance," or "showed consistent effort in playing to his or her capability." Again, the goal is to recognize improvement, effort, and competence in the allocation of any award in youth sport.

In summary, remember that child athletes are not miniature adults. They have fragile personalities, with underdeveloped self-esteem and confidence; they believe everything most adults tell them, especially sports coaches and parents on whom they depend for security, safety, recognition, approval, instruction, and even love. In addition, the level of sports skills of children is relatively low. They are still developing their motor coordination and other abilities (e.g., strength, reaction time, movement speed, hand-eye coordination). Therefore, when a sports coach reprimands a child athlete for making an error or a mistake, especially if it leads to performance failure and defeat, the child is deeply affected; often humiliated and embarrassed. Prolonged adult hostility toward the child athlete often results in the child quitting the sport altogether, and often never playing any sport again. Considering the dropout rate of close to 70% of child athletes under age 14 years, adults can do better at managing the child's sport experience. One factor that contributes to reduced IM due to allocating trophies is called *the overjustification effect.*

It is well known that the primary reason children play sport is to have fun. Kids do not ask for trophies; however, adults feel the need to give them out, either selectively as a reward for competent performance or to everyone who participates on the team. So, we can assume that unless a child is being forced to play sports, perhaps by an overzealous parent, child athletes are already intrinsically motivated to play. Adults, however, do not seem to agree that children are just fine without receiving rewards in response to their performance attainment, either individually or collectively as a team; remember, we are talking *youth* sports—under age 14 years—not adolescents or adults. Many, if not most, youth sports organizations have reward giving as an integral part of their program. This assumption is flawed based on studies on the effectiveness of rewards on motivation among children.

Reliance on rewards is a form of *extrinsic*, not intrinsic, motivation. Play is turned into work. Here is the problem: According to the prevailing research (see Anshel, 2012, for a review of this literature), play, including sport, is intrinsically motivating for children. Kids love to play, even without an external motive, such as a trophy, money, clothing, and so on—at least normally. It is the role of adults, including parents and sports coaches, to increase children's IM and prevent or at least reduce EM (external motivation). The questions must be asked are (1) Does the use of rewards undermine IM? and (2) Do children want or need rewards to enjoy their sports participation? Is the adult community actually undermining the child athletes' IM by installing a reward system that child athletes do not need and, perhaps, that gets in the way of playing sports for enjoyment?

The effect of an award on IM and EM is directly related to how the child perceived the reason for the award. If a child's motivation for engaging in an activity goes from internal (e.g., fun) to external (e.g., the trophy or some other tangible award), the child's IM is being undermined. This process is called the *overjustification effect* (Lepper, Greene, & Nesbitt, 1973). This effect occurs when the child receives an award that is expected and highly recognized—not just a pat on the back but a highly visible reward such as a trophy. The overjustification is based on adult assumptions that children cannot possibly want to participate in an activity for pleasure. Adults overjustify their children's reasons for engaging in the activity by making an erroneous assumption that they do not have the incentive to play sports in the absence of some tangible reward. While rewards *can* increase IM under specific circumstances (see Anshel, 2012, pp. 65–66, for a review of this material), IM *decreases* when child athletes view the award as the primary reason to compete. Further participation in sport will likely stop if an award is expected but not provided. This phenomenon is one reason for the excessive sports dropout and supports the claims of proponents who claim that giving a trophy or some other award to all participants will reduce the high rate of sport dropout in youth sports. Thus, instead of arguing who receives and does not receive an end-of-season trophy, the overjustification effect suggests that no one should receive one. Just let the kids play and have fun.

The messages coming from child psychologists and researchers about having our children develop healthy attitudes toward handling inevitable—and desirable—experiences of failure are as follows: (1) If you are a parent, allow your children the dignity of doing things for themselves when possible. (2) If you are a teacher, make an effort to help parents of students know what age-appropriate responsibilities are for their children. Don't expect that parents already know. And (3), if a parent is doing something for their children that they (children) could do for themselves, the parent is enabling them and setting them up for some difficult days ahead in life. According to columnist Susan Steen (2015, p. 2D), "Success is a wonderful thing to enjoy, but how can you appreciate it if you've never not succeeded? How can you know a great chocolate chip cookie if you haven't burned a few batches to be able to compare?"

10

HANDLING FAILURE IN SPORT SETTINGS

Be of good cheer. Do not think of today's failures, but of the success that may come tomorrow. You have set yourself a difficult task, but you will succeed if you persevere; and you will find a joy in overcoming obstacles.

—Helen Keller, 1880–1968, blind and
deaf educator (Cook, 1993, p. 246)

Sport competition would not exist if it weren't for failure. Failed performance is inherent to sport because competition mandates failure as part of the process of comparing the skill level and competence of two or more individuals. The comparison will lead to an outcome that categorizes the individuals or groups as the "winner" and the "loser." As Alderman (1974) explains, "In direct competition, people struggle against each other in a clearly personal context . . . each performer attempts to maximize his success while at the same time minimizing that of his opponents. . . . Winning thus replaces excellence as the main value of competition in sport" (p. 75). Thus, competitive sport mandates what Alderman calls a "zero-sum type of competition, i.e., competition wherein one competitor wins and the other loses" (p. 75). Whichever team fails least, wins. Integrating failure in sport also seems appropriate—even necessary—given the challenges of encouraging children and adolescents to maintain sport participation and avoid dropping out so that they remain physically active and perform sport skills over their lifetime. This chapter addresses how to integrate failure at all levels of competitive sport and how to help athletes deal with failure constructively so that it is a learning tool and is perceived by athletes as a stepping-stone to success.

Failure is a vehicle for increased incentive to overcome barriers to begin and maintain sports participation, to feel comfortable with the process of learning sport skills, and to apply cognitive and behavioral strategies to make failure a source of motivation and a foundation factor in the process of skill mastery and performance success.

There are two important components of linking failure with performance success in sport. The first component is to recognize our *humanness as imperfect organisms* and that errors, mistakes, misunderstandings, misperceptions, disappointment, and finally, failure outcomes are an integral part of the human condition. In the words of Hall of Fame baseball great Mickey Mantle, "During my 18 years I came to bat almost 10,000 times. I struck out about 1,700 times and walked maybe 1,800 times. You figure a ballplayer will average about 500 at-bats a season. That means I played seven years in the major leagues without even hitting the ball" (Lesyk, 2004, p. 27).

The second component is *self-awareness* about how we react to mistakes in sport settings and how to improve on that reaction (discussed in greater length later in this chapter). That is, we need to establish a firm foundation about how we actually cope with failure versus how we *should* cope with failure in sport (Ravizza, 2015).

In his book, *Men at Work* (1990), about the complexities of major league baseball, author George Will discloses an interview with former major league player and manager Jim Lefebvre: "There are several guys in this league—I mean *stars*—who have their routines. As soon as you break their routines, they get uncomfortable. So we try to figure ways to do that" (p. 25).

PROPER EXPECTATIONS (NOT FEAR) OF FAILURE

The old adage "practice makes perfect" has done incredible harm to all sports participants, not because practice and the outcomes from practice are unimportant, but because it—the concept of practice makes perfect—creates inappropriate and inaccurate expectations of success. The phrase suggests that the more we practice, the more likely it is that we will succeed and perform sport skills flawlessly—no matter how complex the skill. Nothing can be further from the truth. Practice can be conducted properly, following sound principles of teaching motor skills, a science called *sport pedagogy* or *motor behavior*, or improperly in which coaches can require athletes to engage in overtraining, sometimes leading to chronic stress, burnout, and often quitting sport altogether.

Failure can be categorized as successful, positive, and constructive *if* the sports competitor uses the experiences from failed or disappointing outcomes to increase the chance of future success. Highly confident athletes build their future success from past failures, and that includes every elite athlete in the world. Success in sport is highly unlikely without first experiencing some degree of failure, including thoughts of quitting sport altogether. "Positive failure" means that athletes arrive at practice expecting to make mistakes, both physical and mental, which are communicated in the form of information (verbal or visual) feedback and make us better.

Failure categorized as unsuccessful, negative, stressful, and destructive, on the other hand, is based on expecting performance perfection, but experiencing a performance level that falls below wishful thinking and hoping. This breeds disappointing performance outcomes, leading to frustration, stress, anger, and/or resignation (e.g., "I'm just not good enough"). Not surprisingly, performance results often fall below the athlete's expectations, and they are unable to cope with what has been labeled "poor" performance. The result is experiencing heightened stress, anxiety, and pressure applied by coaches, spectators (including those who are recruiting elite performers), and perhaps the media and parents, as reflected by this actual (sad) story.

Bill was a 13-year-old highly skilled swimmer living in Montreal, Quebec, Canada. His swimming skills led to Bill being considered a future Canadian Olympic swimmer. Bill's father escorted him to swim practice several times a week. I was guarding the outdoor pool on this particular late afternoon when Bill and his father walked into the facility, consisting of a 10-lane Olympic-sized pool. Bill quickly entered the water and completed a lap to slowly warm up, while his father watched from the side. Bill's father then instructed his son to swim 10 laps of the pool. Without hesitating Bill started swimming. After completing the laps, Bill complained of fatigue. His father would hear none of that. He told his son the following: "*If you want daddy to love you, you will swim two final laps at full speed*. That's what it takes to be an Olympic swimmer." Bill looked down in apparent disappointment but obeyed his father's instructions. He started his final two-lap swim at sprint speed.

Sadly, Bill's father was using *conditional love* by stating that his love for his son was contingent on his son's completion of laps in the pool. A parent's or coach's conditional love increases anxiety in the athlete or child due to the perception that only meeting expectations of adults will result in much-needed recognition, approval, and love. Sometimes adult expectations are perceived by children or athletes as excessive; they may supersede the child's ability to meet those expectations, especially if the child's perceived ability is below that of the parent or coach.

Bill quit swimming at age 15, never approaching his parents' expectations of him swimming in the Olympic Games. Worse, the swimmer stopped all forms of physical activity, never returned to the water, and had a drug problem for many months that almost ended his life. This swimmer's father was relentless in maintaining extraordinary expectations for his son who eventually burned out and quit the sport the father was hoping would lead to Olympic glory—a lost opportunity in which failure led to a young athlete's loss of self-identity.

SELF-AWARENESS AND RESPONDING TO FAILURE: WHO ARE WE WHEN WE FAIL?

How do highly skilled athletes react to and cope with failure? Do they actively process the experience so that they can learn from it and use what they learn to perform better in the future? Or do they lose emotional control, expect to perform at the highest level at all times, and maintain negative thoughts and emotions? How do elite athletes respond to failure, as opposed to their less skilled, often younger counterparts? Highly skilled athletes who acknowledge and confront their emotional reactions to disappointing and undesirable performance engage in a process called self-awareness. Self-awareness is the stepping-stone toward experiencing successful failure.

Self-awareness, according to Dr. Ken Ravizza (2015), who has consulted with professional athletes for many years, is the athlete's willingness to "check in" and determine if his or her arousal level, emotional state, thought processes, and focus are where they need to be and, if not, adjust them to give the best opportunity for success.

Self-awareness has also been defined as *self-monitoring*—in which the athlete consciously gathers information or tracks either desirable or undesirable behaviors—that leads to desirable, targeted performance outcome, let's say "number of errors moving to the right" or "performing poorly in pressure situations." *Self-awareness*, then, is an athlete's willingness to become cognizant of how her actions affect herself or affects others, then using this information constructively to increase the chances of future success. The ways in which coaches and athletes define and react to—cope with—perceived failure directly influence its potential benefits.

MOVING FORWARD WITH POSITIVE FAILURE

There is a line in the theatrical production of *Les Misérables* that goes, "It is nothing to die. It is an awful thing never to have lived." When we deny our internal flaws, bury them, and then pretend they do not exist, we have never lived. Athletes who reach—or attempt to reach—their performance potential willingly face their flaws whenever possible, at least within the context of sport competition. It's a process called *positive failure*. Author John C. Maxwell (2000) suggests using the following strategies for moving ahead following failure (adapted for sports competitors):

1. *See yourself clearly.* To reach their potential, athletes need to "look inside" and observe all the bad and all the good. It is wrong to see only flaws while denying the good, or see only the good while denying the

flaws. A more balanced perspective is needed so that one's perspective of his or her talent is accurate.

2. *Admit your flaws honestly.* Athletes who are defensive and refuse to be held accountable for their actions, especially actions that lead to undesirable consequences, fail to grow and mature. They do not get better. Instead, they often remain emotionally immature because they have refused to take responsibility for their actions and learn from their mistakes. Elite-level athletes take responsibility for the quality of their athletic performance. This includes acknowledging—even celebrating—their limitations so they understand what they can and cannot do.

3. *Discover your strengths.* Athletes cannot achieve their dreams working outside of their area of expertise. To excel, athletes need to do what they do very well; acknowledge and practice within their strengths, but strive to get better outside their comfort zone.

4. *Build on those strengths.* Athletes improve if they enthusiastically develop their natural talents and abilities. They must remain dedicated to changing themselves if they are to change the world. Using failure as a vehicle for change accomplishes that result; eventually their failures become successes.

The sport psychology literature is clear about what separates elite versus nonelite athletes: The difference between average and above-average (high-achieving) athletes is their perception of and response to failure. Elite athletes have a strong desire to achieve and to accomplish their goals. As former Los Angeles Dodger first baseman Steve Garvey has said, "You have to set the goals that are almost out of reach. If you set a goal that is attainable without much work or thought, you are stuck with something below your true talent and potential" (Lesyk, 2004, p. 44).

Perhaps the key issue surrounding failure in sport is not whether athletes will experience it; they will. *All* athletes do. Rather, good failure is about how they *respond* to it. Looking beyond failure is another way of saying that we need to effectively deal with it. We must look beyond failure and use it to eventually achieve our goals, hopes, and dreams.

HOW SPORTS COACHES CAN BUILD A MENTALLY SAFE TEAM CLIMATE

Sports team members need to feel comfortable in reporting possible and actual problems and failures. Coaches, in turn, should make it safe for players to report their observations and opinions. Here are five strategies for building a *mentally safe environment* to protect the value of experiencing failure.

1. Help Athletes Understand the Possible Issues and Problems

What kinds of errors and failures can be expected to occur before and during the contest? Is the field soggy yet playable? Is a segment of the field uneven lending itself to tripping while running in that area? Is performing a certain strategy prone to performance error? Have certain skills and strategies been sufficiently practiced that they can be performed under competitive conditions? Sports events are sometimes won or lost due to a series of small events and strategies that did not work out as planned. Team leaders can spread knowledge and understanding of reducing error and the chance of failure.

2. Reward Whistleblowers

There is considerable knowledge among team members about what strategies are working well and which ones are not. Athletes and other team members should be encouraged to inform management about bad news, expressing concerns, asking questions, or detecting mistakes. They should be rewarded rather than criticized, cut from the team, or demoted to non-starting status.

One approach to better utilize the experiences and knowledge of team members is to establish a program called *blameless reporting*. Team members should be encouraged to reveal detected errors, mistakes, and failed strategies *anonymously*. Reports of problems should not be handwritten, so that management can identify the writer, although identifying the writer allows for further probing of the relevant issues and fixing the problem. What errors are being reported, and what is the process of responding to this feedback?

For 10 weeks I conducted in-service training to emergency dispatchers (the folks who answer 9-1-1 calls) on improving their skills related to coping with stress (see Anshel, Umscheid, & Brinthaupt, 2013, for a description of this program and the associated study). The dispatchers complained about numerous issues but were especially critical about the lack of leadership in the unit. There was no in-service training of dispatchers, no open communication with police department administration, poor relationships among the dispatchers, and a lack of morale. While a description of this study goes beyond the scope of this chapter, of importance here is the need to allow and be receptive to input from subordinates about improvements and other needed changes for creating better service. Subordinates often know more about the program and the operation than most administrators of the same program. Regularly scheduled interactions between supervisor and subordinates are almost always needed for a more efficient operation.

3. Be Open About What You Do Not Know

Team members are very empathetic toward coaches (and other administrators) who share their stories of imperfections, errors, regrets, and struggles, rather than appearing to have led error-free, perfect lives, impervious to pain, challenges, and other difficulties. Athletes want to learn from the mistakes of others who turned around their career to lead highly productive lives and successful careers. Effective coaches are open about what they do not know, mistakes they have made, and what is impossible to accomplish without the help of others—coaches, players, other team personnel. Rarely is the Lone Ranger leader successful in charging ahead all alone.

4. Ask for Observations and Ideas

Create opportunities for team members to detect and analyze failures, and promote well-thought-out attempts to understand the source of the problem. Does a certain athlete perform better under some circumstances than others? Athletes who do not deal well with pressure might perform better at certain positions or under specific (nonthreatening) conditions. Is Player A better than Player B under pressure, perhaps due to a mental limitation or a condition of the competition (e.g., audience activity, opponent intimidation, noise). Invite participation by all team members, particularly assistant coaches, to address issues they have observed or predicted, or about which they have concerns.

5. Clarify What Acts Are Blameworthy—Sometimes Finding Fault Is Helpful

Do some team members feel more secure and safe when informed about what actions are blameworthy—actions that are linked to consequences? Performers learn from errors that are explained by blame. The consequences of a blameworthy issue, however, should be nonthreatening and not result in being cut from the team. The exception to that would be if the law was broken, an error led to serious injury, or the person repeatedly made the same mistakes. What can be learned from this undesirable experience? To use a cliché, the punishment should fit the crime. Perhaps an athlete is missing practice for no valid reason. Some athletes are negative and critical of the team, and go around blaming the coach or teammates for the team's failures. Perhaps an athlete is making the same mistake repeatedly, leading to losing the contest. All of these examples might be "blameworthy" if the complainer offered specific examples of situations that support the complaint and this is communicated in private with a team leader/coach/captain.

THE ART AND SCIENCE OF SPORT ALTRUISM: HELPING OTHERS FIRST

Sports teams are groups, and researchers tell us that groups are more effective when they are cohesive—feel and act with a sense of togetherness—a concept called team cohesion. One of the most effective ways to improve team cohesion is to make sure that all group members are viewed as important to group functioning and supported by others in the group, especially after the inevitable experience of individual and group failure. Study after study indicates that the greatest source of joy and happiness among most of us is altruism—giving our time and energy to the benefit of others.

The Value of Social Support as an Antidote to Sport Failure

As indicated earlier, failure in competitive sport is inevitable. The challenge for athletes and their coaches is not so much to strive to prevent failure; humans are inherently imperfect and, therefore, susceptible to errors and mistakes. But what sports participants can do is to "fail productively," what Tavis Smiley (2011) calls "failing up." "Failure," he claims, "is an inevitable part of the human journey. . . . When you take the time to learn your lessons, when you use those lessons as stepping-stones to climb even higher than you were before, you transcend failure—you fail up" (p. xvii). Failing up is a challenging process in competitive sport because failure is inherent to eventual success. Success through failure in sport is a marathon event, not a sprint, and definitely not easily accomplished alone. The athlete needs collaboration with teammates and coaches on this journey. The process of positive interactions with teammates, thereby reducing the intensity and frequency of experiencing unpleasant feelings from sport failure, is called social support, more informally referred to as "watching my back."

Social support refers to giving comfort, assistance, and/or information to others. Researchers who measure the effects of social support on changes in behavior and emotion have categorized five main types of social support, all of which are related to dealing with overcoming and dealing constructively with sport failure.

Instrumental support consists of providing tangible and practical assistance that will help teammates meet their goals. Throwing batting practice, playing catch or warming up (e.g., stretches, performing precontest routines), providing transportation, or even keeping in touch between competitive events are sample forms of instrumental support.

Emotional support entails expressing encouragement, empathy, and/ or concern toward a person. The purpose of emotional support is to help teammates manage negative emotions and to maintain effort and positive emotions. Praising a teammate for his/her efforts; encouraging him/her to work harder, to "keep trying" and hang in there and not give up after making an error; and maintaining adherence to a teammate's rehabilitation program are examples.

Informational support includes proving teammates or coaches with advice, suggestions, or directions that pertain to improving some segment of the team, the individual athlete, or a component of the contest. Athletes are not mannequins. They have insights, past experience, skills, and an understanding of performance strategy that can—and should—be shared with others at the appropriate time.

Companionship support reflects the availability of teammates, coaches, team member partners, and other team support staff (e.g., physical therapist, counselor/psychologist, team physician, conditioning coach) for personal discussions, review of team/contest strategy, improving physical or mental readiness for the contest, training/working out together, or addressing and, hopefully, overcoming a problem or concern.

Validation support involves comparing oneself to others in order to measure progress or to validate that one's thoughts, feelings, problems, and perceptions are accurate and appropriate. Often, teams will have more than one athlete able to demonstrate proper skills in a specific position (i.e., team substitutes, or second string). Some starting positions on a team may be competitive, so it's important to inform players of the reasons certain players are starting, while others are substitutes—or that players are given specific roles during certain phases of the contest. Examples include special teams in football, substitute base running in baseball, or filling in for injured players in all sports.

Sport failure is embarrassing, humiliating, distracting, upsetting, and often leads to quitting. Post-retirement from sport can be accompanied by chronic pain and the need for rehabilitation and counseling. All team members need support of various kinds so that failure is not devastating and damaging to the athlete. Positive failure means the athlete is driven to consider the needs of his or her teammates, that is, thinking about the welfare of others, being a good teammate by helping other team members, including nonstarters and team member nonplayers, whenever possible.

Media stories over the years have clearly indicated that some well-known and highly successful athletes would mentor younger, less experienced novice athletes, while other elite-level athletes would ignore them and focus exclusively on their own contest preparation and performance. It is desirable to reduce your burden of looking after your own needs first, and put others—teammates, family, spectators, disabled veterans, hospital patients—ahead of you in developing team member (group) cohesion and a sense of mutual support.

FINAL COMMENTS FOR THIS CHAPTER

As indicated earlier, failure is a perception. The grading system in many school systems ranges from E or A (excellent) to F (failure). Elementary school children are introduced to failure in a threatening manner in settings that assess academic performance. Receiving an F indicates the student's inability to master even half the material based on an array of grading criteria. Receiving an F is to be feared; there are punitive repercussions to be experienced—at home and school. It is necessary, therefore, for children to "unlearn" how they perceive the label, or category, of failure and to create a new, more appealing view of failure that makes it less threatening and undesirable, and more integrated into a constructive (elite) category related to learning, improving, and achieving.

Failure in sport is about pursuing excellence, not winning or perfection. According to decathlon champion Daley Thompson, "My enjoyment obviously comes from winning, but more than anything else it comes from performing well" (Lesyk, 2004, p. 6). And writer Pearl S. Buck has said, "The secret of joy in work is contained in one word—*excellence*. To know how to do something well is to enjoy it" (Lesyk, 2004, p. 8). Athletes are unequivocal in their collective view that giving one's best—optimal effort and the struggle for high-quality and consistent performance outcomes—is not about winning or perfection. It is about attempts at perfection. The late football coach Vince Lombardi said it best as he addressed his team, the Green Bay Packers: "Listen, I know you can't be perfect. But boys, making the effort to be perfect, trying as hard as you can is what life is all about" (Lesyk, 2004, p. 11).

Hall of Fame baseball player Henry "Hank" Aaron was the first player to break Babe Ruth's career home run record (755), a record that was subsequently broken by Barry Bonds in 2007. Aaron hit only 13 home runs in his rookie year and struck out a particularly high 1,294 times over his career with the Milwaukee/Atlanta Braves and Milwaukee Brewers. Bonds also had a very high strikeout rate. Despite their respective stellar home run totals, both players struggled to hit major league pitching early in their career and, like many home run hitters, had a high failure (strikeout) rate. Aaron's ability to deal with failure led to an outstanding career and entry into baseball's Hall of Fame.

Experiencing failure, which guarantees imperfection, is an integral part of the journey toward achieving excellence. The elites are consistently unwilling to settle for anything less than attempts at excellence in all areas of life.

11

HANDLING FAILURE
IN EXERCISE SETTINGS

Happy are those who dream dreams and are ready to pay the price to make them come true.

—Leo Jozef Suenens, 1904–1996, clergyman
(Cook, 1993, p. 468)

Perhaps there is no single habit or routine at which we, as a collective society, *fail* more often and so widespread than daily exercise and other forms of physical activity. Starting and maintaining an exercise program is like asking someone to give up their favorite foods or to adopt a new religion. It's very challenging and difficult to institute a new exercise habit. For over 30 years, I have observed the same problems and challenges of getting people to become physically active, and the medical problems of leading a sedentary lifestyle have not abated. We continue to fight the "battle of the bulge," although there is evidence that people are becoming more aware of the consequences of their unhealthy eating and low-activity habits.

The fitness industry is dedicated to helping a person begin and maintain a regularly scheduled habit of exercise, a process called *adherence*. While the fitness industry has tried to recruit and maintain its membership all over the country—it is, after all, a business and needs member income to survive—it has generally failed to achieve widespread exercise adherence.

Reasons for starting and then quitting exercise program abound. Here are the main reasons for dropping out of exercise programs.

EXERCISE BARRIERS: WHY WE START AND THEN STOP OUR EXERCISE HABIT

Dropping out of a group exercise program or quitting our personal exercise regimen has been a serious concern among fitness leaders, fitness club owners, and researchers. Sadly, approximately 50% of exercise participants stop exercising *in structured programs* within the first 6 months of starting, although researchers are uncertain if any of these individuals continue to exercise on their own.

With all of the attention, time, and energy that fitness club owners and staff have given to fostering lifelong exercise habits, it's sad when a person finally commits to exercise and then quits. Even when a doctor prescribes a formal, supervised exercise rehabilitation program, some individuals will not maintain this habit. Why does this happen? Is the fitness industry to blame? Have researchers and practitioners failed to detect the "true" reasons for a person's decision to discontinue an exercise habit? Although novice exercisers often need more encouragement in these programs than they are receiving, exercisers may also make several errors in technique that increase discomfort and exertion, and reduce progress.

The primary causes of dropping out of exercise programs, called *perceived exercise barriers*, include lack of time, experiencing pain/discomfort/injury, fear of injury, unavailable exercise equipment or facility, lack of knowledge about proper exercise technique, finding exercise unpleasant, lack of confidence, feeling intimidated, no exercise partner, lack of support from partner/others, history of giving up, too expensive, and no close access to a facility. These exercise barriers are called "perceived" because they are based on the individual's (survey respondent's) personal explanations and interpretation of reasons for not exercising. They may not, in fact, be based on reality.

The Most Common Exercise Barrier: Not Enough Time

Let's take the most common reason given for not exercising: *not enough time*. People who quit their exercise program due, ostensibly, to insufficient time usually perceive their schedule as too demanding and too busy to find *three hours per week* for strenuous physical activity.

Is the "not enough time" claim valid? Let's do the math. There are 168 hours in a week (24 hours/day x 7 days/week). Results from the scientific (exercise physiology) literature indicates that to achieve cardiovascular fitness a person should exercise at least three times (hours) per week, preferably every other day. Three hours out of 168 hours per week is equal to 0.017% of the week. That means that fitness can be achieved by engaging in aerobic exercise less than 2% of a person's time over one full week. That's only a fraction of the time we talk on our cell phone (about 9% to 12% of our week), watch television (10% to 15%), and drive in our cars (6% to 9% for people who work full time). In other words, the lack-of-time excuse is perception but not reality, especially if a person schedules exercise sessions each week and considers exercise a long-term investment in good health, weight control, enjoyment, socializing, more energy, and higher quality of life. The key issue in overcoming exercise barriers is to develop and maintain an exercise program that targets each perceived barrier. Additional benefits of regular exercise are psychological, such as reduced stress and anxiety, higher confidence, prevention of and help in overcoming depression, and higher-quality sleep.

EXERCISE INTERVENTIONS

The exercise psychology literature has focused on the best strategies to encourage individuals to start and maintain an exercise habit and prevent exercise failure. Lox, Ginis, and Petruzzello (2014) categorize exercise interventions into four approaches:

1. *Informational* (increasing the exerciser's knowledge about fitness benefits and techniques)
2. *Behavioral* (e.g., setting short-term and long-term goals, self-monitoring, keeping records, fitness testing, exercising to music)

3. *Social* (e.g., promoting social support by exercising in a group or as partners, establishing group or family exercise programs)
4. *Environmental policy* (e.g., providing walking trails, community centers, bicycle paths, mandatory physical education classes in schools)

Social support is among the most powerful forms of exercise satisfaction, pleasure, and achievement because most of us thrive in the company of others. We love having our own cheering section, especially when it comes to overcoming the challenges of developing an exercise routine and the typical discomfort that comes with physical exertion. Social support, then, concerns the influence of others in improving our exercise motivation, performance, and adherence to our program.

There are five types of social support: instrumental, emotional, informational, companionship, and validation. Most of us incorporate some—perhaps all—of these into our lifestyle to complete our mission of regular exercise to improve our fitness and health.

1. *Instrumental social support*: This involves providing hands-on, practical assistance that will help exercisers achieve their goals. Examples include transporting exercisers to their exercise program, spotting a weightlifter during exertion in the weight room, providing babysitting services so that parents may exercise, or temporarily taking a work colleague's responsibilities.
2. *Emotional social support*: This kind occurs when the support person demonstrates encouragement, caring, empathy, and concern toward others. Examples include praising exercisers for their effort, commitment, and improvement for attempting to reach or actually achieving their fitness goals, or by providing empathy in response to a person's discomfort, fatigue, or injury in their efforts to improve fitness and improve health.
3. *Informational social support*: This area concerns giving advice, instructions, directions, suggestions, or feedback about the exerciser's progress. Health practitioners and fitness trainers are *primary/formal* sources of informational support for exercise. *Secondary/informal* sources include family and friends who can share their personal story about how they achieved better health through exercise, or by provid-

ing tips about how they overcame obstacles for building rituals that allowed them to maintain an active lifestyle.

4. *Companionship social support*: This type concerns the availability of people with whom one can exercise, such as a friend, family member, or exercise group—an exercise buddy. Exercising with a companion can provide positive feelings and increased motivation, and can distract the exerciser from the challenges of physical exertion, such as fatigue, discomfort, or boredom. Of course, some people prefer to exercise alone, and there is no harm in that. In fact, feeling forced or even encouraged to exercise with others when exercising alone is preferred can reduce, not increase, the benefits of social support.

5. *Validation social support*: Sometimes we need to compare our exercise performance or our physical features with others either during or between exercise sessions. For some people, interpersonal comparisons confirm that their struggles to reduce weight or improve fitness are shared by others. Favorable comparisons also encourage and motivate exercisers. The self-talk may consist of "If he can take off all that weight, so can I." Exercising in groups whose members have similar characteristics, such as programs in cardiac rehabilitation or obesity reduction, provides a sense of comradery. Discussing common challenges and goals in the desire to establish and maintain a healthy lifestyle is encouraged.

Researchers have found that the benefits of social support are greater for less fit, novice exercisers than for fitter, more advanced exercisers who are usually highly self-motivated to maintain their exercise habit. In addition, women seem to benefit from various forms of social support more so than men, although both sexes experience similar benefits in *group* programs related to rehabilitation, weight control, or people with special needs.

Social support is effective only if exercisers surround themselves with people who are positive, optimistic, encouraging, caring, and sensitive to their needs. The key word in applying this strategy is *support*, not criticism. We demonstrate our love and respect for others, especially to our family, by *supporting* them in their mission to improve health, energy, and quality of life. This is how we say to those we value, "I love you."

All of these areas form an important role in the "war on obesity" and are ways to increase physical activity rates in a sedentary, overweight society. We will use some of these intervention categories in the following section on overcoming common exercise errors.

DISCONNECTED VALUES (INTERVENTION) MODEL

Changing habits, even if they are self-destructive (e.g., lack of exercise, overeating, poor sleep patterns) and a danger to good health and happiness, is a challenging process. This is because habits and routines, such as the lack of regular exercise, are firmly entrenched in the person's lifestyle. A habit that is intended to increase exercise behavior is particularly difficult because in addition to making the time for this new habit, there is also the challenge of overcoming years of negative attitudes and feelings toward exercise, partly due to unpleasant past experiences and overcoming the discomfort of physical exertion (Anshel, 2014). The degree of discomfort is usually related to the person's current body weight, the degree of poor fitness, and other unhealthy lifestyle habits. Anshel (2008) has developed a health behavior change intervention that has been shown to effectively replace unhealthy habits with more desirable, healthier rituals. It's called the Disconnected Values Model (DVM).

The DVM is predicated on the postulate that human self-motivated behavior is a function of developing habits that are consistent with the person's core values and beliefs about what is really important, that is, about which he or she feels most passionate (see Anshel, 2008, 2013, for a complete and in-depth review of the model). Behavior is sustained by a person's continued attempts to build and maintain rituals that support his or her values and beliefs.

With respect to developing an exercise habit, a person who exercises regularly also reflects values such as family because they will have more energy and lead a higher quality of life in meeting the needs of family members. Perhaps, then, the DVM predicts that the self-motivation to develop an exercise habit rests, at least in part, on recognizing the inconsistency between one's negative habits (i.e., lack of regular exercise) and one's values, and then to institute a new, positive habit of exercise that is strongly connected to one's values. The DVM has been shown to significantly improve health-related behaviors (Anshel, 2013; Anshel, Kang, & Brinthaupt, 2010). In one study, Anshel, Brinthaupt, and Kang (2010) found that the DVM improved mental well-being after a 10-week exercise program.

One likely factor that explains the effectiveness of this model is that, in addition to making changes in exercise habits, participants also incorporated lifestyle changes. A person's adherence to improving health-related behaviors is usually accompanied by recognizing their long-term benefits and developing new rituals that create new, healthy habits. Hall and Fong (2003) found that "long-term thinkers (i.e., persons who are capable of delaying short-term gratification) are more likely than short-term thinkers to engage in health-protective behaviors and less likely to engage in health-damaging behaviors" (p. 685).

The outcomes of past DVM studies have also indicated a relatively low exercise dropout rate. In the Anshel, Kang, and Brinthaupt (2010) study, only 11% of the participants who began the program and received preintervention fitness tests indicated they had stopped exercising prior to postintervention tests. Their self-reported reasons for dropping out (e.g., not enough time, injury or pain, unable to make appointed times for coaching) are common exercise barriers. Perhaps the most plausible explanation for the low dropout rate in studies employing the DVM comes from Dominick and Morey (2006), who offer a list of strategies to enhance exercise adherence that are integrated into the DVM. These strategies include providing exercise participants with "a convenient time and location, reasonable cost, variety of exercise modalities, flexibility in exercise goals, and quality of the exercise leader" (p. 61). The perceived expertise and communication skills of exercise leaders are especially valuable for promoting adherence and preventing dropout. For example, participants in the Anshel, Kang, and Brinthaupt (2010) study repeatedly indicated, on postprogram evaluation forms, that one reason they maintained participation in the program was feelings of loyalty to their fitness coach. As Dominck and Morey (2006) suggest, "Exercise leaders should be able to effectively educate participants about physical activity and to motivate participants to continue exercising using a variety of strategies" (p. 61).

Another possible reason for the positive outcomes in the Anshel, Kang, and Brinthaupt (2010) study, often ignored in health behavior change research, was the opportunity to build secure and trusting relationships between participants and their performance (i.e., fitness and nutrition) coaches. Health care professionals (e.g., fitness trainers, registered dieticians) need to create an environment that will facilitate health behavior change. Fitness professionals are the best sources of primary prevention because they provide an environment that has less of a medical focus and is more closely associated with lifestyle change and wellness. Properly trained professionals provide emotional as well as educational and physical fitness support to clients and remain updated on developing knowledge in the area in which they provide counsel (e.g., exercise, nutrition). These professional relationships that become partly personal will result in improved adherence to healthy habits.

Steps of the DVM: Preventing Exercise Failure (Dropout)

Applying the DVM to change health behavior—that is, replacing unhealthy habits with more desirable, healthier routines—begins with a few motivational comments about our unhealthy habits like lack of exercise: for example, (1) why we do something every day that we *know* is bad for us, (2) the short-term costs (e.g., weight gain) and long-term consequences (e.g., heart disease, stroke, obesity) of no regular exercise, and (3) the goal of all of us to live our life consistent with our values. In the present context, the DVM is for people who want to start and maintain an exercise program. It consists of the following steps (see Anshel, 2008, 2013, and Anshel, Kang, and Brinthaupt, 2010, for more elaborate explanations):

1. Participants identify up to five "negative habits"—and include a list of all habits in the workbook—actions they take almost daily that compromise their happiness, effectiveness, health, and/or quality of life.
2. Participants write out the benefits, costs, and long-term consequences of each negative habit.
3. Participants designate their five most important values taken from a list of 40 values also listed in the workbook.
4. Participants designate a disconnect, or inconsistency, between any of their negative habits and any of their five listed values. I will say

the following: "Look at both lists—negative habits and values. Can you detect an inconsistency between any of them? Do you have a negative habit that is inconsistent, or misaligned, with any of your values? Is there a disconnect between any one or more of your values and your negative habits? For instance, do you value good health, yet you are overweight, do not exercise, and suffer from poor sleep?" All of us likely have at least one disconnect between our habits and values, unless we are in a state of denial.

5. Participants are asked a very important question: "Assuming you found evidence of at least one disconnect between your negative/ unhealthy habits and your values, if you have not already done so, list the short-term costs and long-term consequences of maintaining that negative habit. Is the disconnect acceptable? That is, are the costs and consequences of maintaining the unhealthy habit and continuing to live in a way that is inconsistent with your values acceptable?"

6. Next, participants create an action plan, perhaps guided by their "coach" or group leader. Clients who acknowledge at least one disconnect that is unacceptable should be ready to work on an action plan with a performance coach. The plan might consist of hiring a personal trainer, purchasing fitness clothing or equipment, and scheduling the new habit throughout the week. The client should be ready to embrace at least one new habit that promotes health and quality of life, replacing the old unhealthy habit(s). As Chenoweth (2007) asserts, creating new, healthier habits is more likely if done within the context of making lifestyle changes, which represents the concept of wellness.

7. Participants are asked to follow-up with their program to detect changes in habits and test data. In the program's final stage, participants should compare their preprogram test scores (e.g., fitness tests, blood lipids to detect cholesterol levels, other tests that will change due to lifestyle changes) with posttests at least 12 weeks later, if preprogram test scores were obtained. Participants are asked not to wait too long for posttests because the (hopefully improved) scores can be highly motivating to the exerciser, usually promoting long-term exercise adherence (Anshel, 2014).

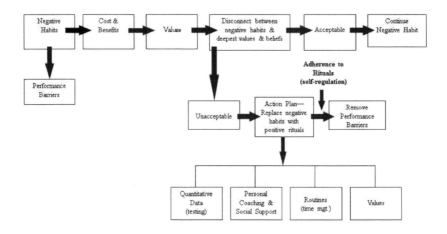

EXERCISE ERRORS AND HOW TO OVERCOME THEM

There are six primary sources of exercise mistakes—or failures—that often lead to performer disappointment, unmet goals, and eventually dropping out (Anshel, 2014).

1. Unrealistic Exercise Goals

You want to lose how many pounds in your first month of starting an exercise program? You want to look like which movie star? Many people are interested in joining an exercise program but do not realize the time needed to overcome decades of past bad habits resulting in poor health and excessive weight. Fitness is a science, so it is important that new exercisers work with a fitness coach—at least at the start of their new program—in determining the best approach to starting and maintaining an exercise program. Let's keep those exercise goals realistic, yet challenging and of moderate difficulty. Similar suggestions are appropriate for the effect of exercise on weight control.

2. Lack of Social Support

Social support consists of the caring, comforting, and assisting an individual receives from others. Social support is especially valuable to novice exercisers in the form of exercising with others, teaching proper exercise and fitness techniques, and providing verbal and nonverbal positive reinforcement—motivational statements support the exerciser's attempts at developing a habit of regular exercise.

3. Lack of Coaching and Instruction

Many highly motivated novice exercisers jump on aerobic or weight equipment or start jogging on the running track without any instruction. Exercisers would be wise to receive extensive instruction on the equipment they plan to use for developing fitness and meeting their exercise goals. While personal coaching can be expensive, if just a few lessons are received, the novice will be able to learn and apply new information about proper exercise technique for life. This is called an investment in one's health and fitness.

4. No Data for Pretesting and Posttesting

People are driven and motivated by data—numbers—that disclose the exerciser's current status at a given period of time and then compare this data set with a follow-up (post) test to determine change, hopefully improvement. It is one thing to be informed that "Your fitness level is low" or "Your blood pressure is a bit high." It is quite another thing, however, to be given the numbers that support the health specialist's words, for example, to be told that your blood pressure is 160 over 100—very high and considered perhaps within the range of being labeled hypertensive. Adherence to exercise is more likely if data sets are obtained and compared.

5. Poor Exercise Technique

There are right ways and wrong ways to exercise. One form of exercise will solicit improved fitness at a faster rate, and fitness goals are more likely to be met sooner. For improving aerobic fitness, it is recommended to engage in interval training.

Interval Training for Improving Aerobic Fitness

An important objective of aerobic exercise is to attain training heart rate (THR). This is an easy calculation: heart rate (HR) should reach 60% to 70% of the person's *predicted*—not actual—maximum HR (i.e., 220 minus age). For a 20-year-old, then, THR would be 220 − 20 = 200 x 0.70 = 140 beats per minute.

The best way to reach THR is through a series of work-rest intervals, rather than engaging in nonstop (continuous) exercise. This is because HR will reach training level when exercise is conducted in a series of relatively brief (2 to 3 minutes), highly intense exercise bouts. Reaching THR strengthens the heart muscle and improves efficiency of the cardiovascular system.

One schedule, for example, would include exercising on a series of work-rest intervals, each consisting of 3 minutes of work (e.g., fast jogging, rapid walking, rapid bicycle pedaling) and 1 minute of rest (not total stopping, but significantly reducing work speed and intensity). More fit individuals can work a bit more and/or rest a bit less. The interval should continue over a period of 20 to 30 minutes because researchers have found that this is the time period needed to strengthen the cardiovascular system. THR will be achieved after "several" work intervals.

Think Time (Minutes), Not Distance (Miles)

Time goals are far easier to achieve than distance goals because the units are more attainable in time (minutes or seconds) than distance (segments of a mile or miles). It is important to reach predetermined goals for improved motivation and a sense of achievement. In addition, the exercise physiology literature addresses time, not distance, as an indicator of improved fitness because time can be controlled and measured much more easily than distance. It is also easier to examine progress against published tables and standards.

6. Failure to Develop an Exercise Habit

The idea behind starting an exercise program is not to end the program after a period of time. The goal is to develop a lifelong exercise habit. This requires working on time management skills to maintain a regular exercise schedule and on exercise routines to perform during the exercise sessions. Developing exercise routines will help ensure familiarity with the fitness program and improve program adherence. Exercise failure—dropping out—is far less likely.

THE ABSTINENCE VIOLATION EFFECT: HOW TO KEEP GOING AFTER EXERCISE FAILURE

The term used to describe a situation in which a person does not resume regular exercise following a temporary halt, or lapse, in exercise or other forms of physical activity is *relapse*. While it is normal to have days in which the person lacks the motivation to exercise for various reasons, frequent exercise lapses can result in a relapse to resuming a sedentary lifestyle. Sometimes an initial lapse leads to the belief that all future hope of improving fitness, losing weight, or experiencing other desirable outcomes is hopeless, resulting in the entire exercise program being abandoned, an all-or-nothing outcome to exercise. A person may go on vacation or become ill or not renew their fitness club membership resulting in weight gain and feeling that all hope is lost on regaining their former level of fitness and body shape. This process is called the *abstinence violation effect*, and it reflects performance failure to maintain an exercise program and concomitant healthy lifestyle (Marlatt & George, 1984).

Reducing the chance of the abstinence violation effect involves reshaping the exerciser's attitude toward missing exercise sessions. Instead of thinking about a lapse as a major problem, which induces feelings of guilt and anxiety, exercisers should view lapses as normal, highly likely, and even as an opportunity to allow one's body to recover from days—even weeks—of strenuous physical activity; a lapse, in other words, is a form of recovery.

Another strategy is to help exercisers form more realistic goals and expectations of their exercise habit. Relatively little fitness is lost if just a few exercise sessions are missed, and the process of "retraining" (i.e., to regain the former fitness level prior to the absence) occurs relatively quickly. This is especially the case if the person's fitness level is relatively high, but even less fit persons need not worry about deficiencies in fitness level. They will regain their fitness level quickly.

EXERCISE ADHERENCE STRATEGIES FOR OVERCOMING EXERCISE BARRIERS

Barriers are inherent to starting and maintaining any new healthy habit—exercise, improved nutrition, coping with stress, and taking recovery breaks, to name a few. Here is some information on ways to combat barriers to the program's number one goal—adhering to your new exercise program. Each of these barriers, although real, is controllable and, therefore, can be managed, according to the research exercise psychology literature (Anshel, 2014).

Not Enough Time

Without question, this is the most common explanation for not exercising—or dropping out after starting a fitness program. Is it realistic? Can we actually run out of time? Answers: (1) The excuse of "no time" is a perception—a person's subjective view of things. It may or may not have anything to do with reality. (2) As mentioned earlier in the chapter, there are 168 hours in a week and if we exercised just three of those hours, which is the minimum that researchers suggest, that would be only *1%* of our total week. (3) Exercise is an investment; a bit less time now to do other things, but much more time to do things later and more efficiently due to more energy. What's your priority when it comes to good health? How about waking up an hour early twice a week for an early morning exercise bout? Perhaps coming home one hour later twice a week due to your exercise routine after work?

Lack of Fitness Information/Knowledge

This is a very common problem, because no one teaches most of us how to exercise correctly. Consequently, our poor form results in discomfort, injury, and lack of effective results. That's why this program has coaching—a lot of it (e.g., fitness, nutrition, mental health, work related). Written materials on fitness may be purchased online or at various bookstores. Newspaper and magazine articles also contain valuable information from experts. Be your own coach. Or hire a personal trainer.

Lack of Confidence

This comes with improvement, mastery of exercise skills (such as weight training, proper use of the machines), and the perception of competence. Most people who are successful have a personality trait called high need achievement. We place ourselves in achievement settings, set challenging goals, and have high self-expectations toward achieving those goals. Therefore, it is natural to feel low confidence (and, therefore, be uncomfortable) in settings in which we are novices or relatively unskilled. As you gain experience and progress in your exercise skills and fitness level, your confidence will increase—dramatically. Confidence is all about task mastery, so stay the course!

Intimidated to Exercise in Public

This issue has been discussed earlier in this chapter. First, most people are too busy exercising to pay attention to you. Second, stop caring what other people think. Stop empowering others to dictate your behavior. Third, the best way to stop thinking about what others think is to develop routines upon entering the exercise venue and keep moving. No need to stop and look around. Stay focused on your own program and the next routine. Working out with a friend is one way to focus on the task at hand and avoid intimidation.

Recruit an Exercise Partner

Tell your fitness coach you are looking for someone with whom to exercise. Your coach can ask around to recruit others who exercise at a similar time and would be pleased to work out with a partner. You can also invite a partner (spouse, friend, work colleague) to exercise with you.

Lack of Support From Partner and Others

This is a tough one. You don't want your desire to get fit, lose weight, and become healthier to be grounds for divorce or losing a friendship. Perhaps your partner is insecure when you are away or thinks that losing weight will result in you becoming "too attractive" to the opposite sex. Insecurity does nasty things to people's minds. Sometimes the unfit partner feels threatened with the improved physical appearance of their fitter partner due to weight loss and musculature. There is a clear lack of support for exercise and fitness. This phenomenon is called *the sabotage effect*. Perhaps professional counseling is needed to determine the reasons your partner or family will not support your wish to exercise. Healthy relationships are based on supporting each other, especially when it comes to increasing energy and improving one's health. Improved physical appearance is also likely. If someone important to you does not want you to exercise, find out the reason(s) and address the causes of this unhealthy attitude.

Here are some ways to gain support from your partner:

1. *Be inclusive.* Try to include your partner in your exercise routine. Exercise together; consider purchasing exercise clothing, equipment, or fitness club memberships as a birthday or holiday gift.
2. *Exercise at home.* Exercise at home with your partner, if possible. This has the benefit of improving exercise adherence because both individuals feel accountable to the other.
3. *Schedule your exercise sessions during the day.* To reduce possible resentment toward you for taking the needed time for your exercise routine, if possible, exercise during the day rather than after work, which would cause you to arrive home late—unless, of course, your partner exercises with you.

History of Giving Up

This is surprisingly common. So many people say, "I tend to stop what I start, anyway, so why even try." Or they will quit exercising when they are forced to temporarily stop, perhaps due to illness, vacation, or injury (a phenomenon called the abstinence relapse effect, discussed earlier). Your body will retrain quickly after stopping temporarily. Do not give up. Also, an exercise partner, personal trainer, goals, meeting social needs, exercising in a comfortable venue (even home), and detecting progress are all ways in which a person can feel reinforced and positive about his or her exercise participation.

Too Expensive

Exercise clothing and equipment make great holiday or birthday gifts, so ask for something (e.g., workout clothes, personal trainer, fitness club membership) or offer gifts that will promote an exercise habit.

No Close Access to an Exercise Facility

Researchers have found that people will not travel more than about three miles out of their way between work and home to attend an exercise facility. If this is your situation, try to exercise at work (if not in a fitness facility, then walk stairs or anywhere you feel safe, do sit-ups in your office, anything that causes you to move), or buy exercise equipment for your home. The reason we tend to ignore our home exercise equipment is because we lack structured routines to use it. In addition, we tend to think of home as a place to relax and spend our time with passive entertainment devices, eating, speaking on the phone, interacting with family, anything but exercise. Equipment collects dust—our promises and New Year's resolutions to the contrary.

Fear of Injury

A fear of injury is not at all uncommon, especially as we age and have a few aches, pain, and previous surgeries and illnesses. So exercise intelligently, with assistance from your physician, personal trainer, and, perhaps, a physical therapist. Be sure to be aware of your physical limitations, but do not avoid movement. Your muscles—including your heart, which is a muscle—need it.

Find Exercise Unpleasant

Many individuals dislike exercising and find exertion unpleasant. We have trained ourselves to be sedentary, so despite the apparent and well-known benefits, exercise is stressful and unpleasant for some people. Some of us also blame our former physical education teachers and sports coaches for our negative attitude toward exercise because they made exercise a form of punishment. The message was therefore ingrained in us that exercise is associated with bad behavior and should be avoided. Physical activity, particularly exercise, does not appeal to many individuals. As we age, however, people who have led a sedentary lifestyle begin to pay the price by experiencing disease, malfunctioning body parts, low energy, poorer health, less happiness, reduced work productivity, and lower quality of life. Part of the reason for a negative attitude toward leading a physically active lifestyle is early experiences as athletes and students in physical education classes. The proliferation of various forms of entertainment and technology has further eroded the joy of physical activity. We spend many hours each week on our electronic devices while forgoing exercise, sport participation, and other forms of active fun and recreation.

THE SELF-MONITORING EXERCISE CHECKLIST
FOR HIGHER FITNESS

Almost 80% of "regular" exercisers have never received formal instruction on correct exercise techniques and procedures. Most people learn to exercise by watching others, reading instructions, or information received from others. Improving physical fitness through exercise, however, is a science. There are right and wrong ways to exercise that influence fitness and other exercise outcomes. For example, exercise techniques for improving cardiovascular (aerobic) fitness are very different from exercises to improve muscular strength. Proper exercise preparation and stretching are also part of one's routine.

One way exercisers can be sure they are consistently doing the right thing when trying to improve their fitness until exercise techniques are learned and feel comfortable is to use a *self-monitoring exercise checklist* (SMEC). The purpose of the SMEC is to provide guidelines for conducting a proper program and listing the correct methods used before, during, and immediately after the exercise session.

The SMEC lists the exerciser's thoughts, emotions, and actions that *should* be done as part of every exercise session. Not everyone has the same exercise needs, goals, and habits, however, so items on the SMEC must be specific to the user. Exercisers may want to add or delete certain items to be compatible with the exerciser's needs. Fitness level should improve and SMEC scores should go higher over a period of weeks. Therefore, current scores should be compared with past scores to make sure proper techniques are mastered and performed consistently.

With time and repetition, these techniques will become habits and be performed automatically. You can find a typical SMEC on page 153.

Self-Monitoring Exercise Checklist

Rate each item, ranging from 1 (*not at all like me*) to 5 (*very much like me*). You may complete this form as often as you wish, but at least once a week. Higher scores are always more desirable. Add or delete items that reflect your own needs.

1	2	3	4	5
Not At All Like Me		Somewhat Like Me		Very Much Like Me

I. Exercise Preparation

1. I think about my exercise sessions with enthusiasm.   1 2 3 4 5
2. I view exercise as a challenge, not a chore.   1 2 3 4 5
3. I know that exercise is good for my health.   1 2 3 4 5
4. I enjoy the company of others during my workout.   1 2 3 4 5
5. I drink plenty (at least four glasses) of water during the day.   1 2 3 4 5
6. I use proper exercise technique (I have received instruction).   1 2 3 4 5
7. I get support from others to exercise regularly.   1 2 3 4 5
8. My exercise sessions are scheduled (days/hours) each week.   1 2 3 4 5
9. I wear the proper shoes and clothing when I exercise.   1 2 3 4 5
10. My exercise shoes and clothing are set aside in advance of my exercise session.   1 2 3 4 5
11. I avoid meals, coffee, and alcohol within two hours before I exercise.   1 2 3 4 5

Total Score:___

II. Pre-exercise Activity (at exercise venue)

1. I arrived at the exercise venue with enthusiasm.   1 2 3 4 5
2. I have an exercise plan before starting.   1 2 3 4 5
3. I remember my exercise and fitness goals.   1 2 3 4 5

4. As I prepare to exercise, I feel energetic.   1   2   3   4   5
5. I plan to have several water breaks before and during the exercise session.   1   2   3   4   5
6. I remember the reasons exercise is good for me.   1   2   3   4   5
7. I complete as much of the exercise session as I can.   1   2   3   4   5
8. I used positive self-talk before my workout. ("I can do it," "I'm ready," "Stay with it!")   1   2   3   4   5
9. I warm up before regular exercise with light aerobic activity (slow jogging).   1   2   3   4   5

Total Score: _____

III. During My Exercise Session

1. I enjoy my exercise session and give 100% effort.   1   2   3   4   5
2. I use positive self-talk while exercising.   1   2   3   4   5
3. I feel good during warm-up and warm-down exercise.   1   2   3   4   5
4. I complete all types of exercises to improve cardio and strength fitness.   1   2   3   4   5
5. I have sufficient resistance on weight machines.   1   2   3   4   5
6. I avoid negative thoughts while exercising.   1   2   3   4   5
7. My exercise performance has improved.   1   2   3   4   5
8. I do not worry about my appearance during exercise.   1   2   3   4   5
9. If I feel tired, I rest briefly and then resume.   1   2   3   4   5
10. I view each exercise bout as a challenge.   1   2   3   4   5
11. During the workout I focus my attention externally, *not* internally, on my fatigue and discomfort.   1   2   3   4   5
12. I try to reach my performance goals.   1   2   3   4   5
13. I sip water during my routine.   1   2   3   4   5

Total Score: _____

IV. After the Exercise Session

1. I am generally pleased with my exercise performance.   1   2   3   4   5
2. I feel that my performance has improved.   1   2   3   4   5

3. I reached my target heart rate (if exercising aerobically).	1	2	3	4	5
4. I drink a lot of water to replenish perspiration.	1	2	3	4	5
5. I plan to maintain my exercise program and stay on my schedule.	1	2	3	4	5

Total Score ____

GRAND TOTAL: ____

THE POWER OF A VALUES-BASED INTERVENTION

The Disconnected Values Model is founded on acknowledging our values and the extent to which our values are inconsistent with our unhealthy habits. What are values and why should they guide our daily behavior? Why are values important for changing health behavior and making failure more tolerable?

Values are core beliefs that guide and motivate behavior. Values also provide standards against which we assess behavior, both desirable and undesirable (Rokeach, 1973). Values promote a person's individuality because everyone differs on their most important values and beliefs about what really matters. For example, as Rokeach contends, a person who values health will tend to develop daily rituals and long-term habits that enhance health and general well-being. According to Hogan and Mookherjee (1981), "values may be one of the most distinguishing characteristics motivating human beings and the likely effects of values on human behavior, beliefs, and attitudes are indisputable" (p. 29).

The strength of this model is the recognition that a person's values guide their behavior, and that sharing values with others has a strong effect on the commitment to sacrifice personal, self-serving needs for the benefit of others (e.g., the sports team, the company, family members). One important implication of this model in exercise settings is that a person's values may or may not be compatible with the values of the team's coach, teammates, family members, partners, friends, or an employer. The DVM in this chapter focuses on detecting discord between the individual's values and the negative habit of inactivity. This is particularly relevant when addressing the values of health, happiness, family, and, often, faith—fundamental tenets of quality of life.

Why are values so important when dealing with failure and changing behavior? Values are more central determinants of behavior than are interests and attitudes (Super, 1995), the latter of which are more situational and derived from a core set of values. Thus, a plethora of interests and attitudes are derived from a relatively reduced number of values. In addition, interests, attitudes, and needs are transitory; once satiated, they may not influence behavior. Values, on the other hand, are almost always firmly entrenched and stable; therefore, they transcend situations and guide behavior over a long period of time, especially when it comes to dealing with failure. It is plausible to surmise that values predict behavior (Hogan & Mookherjee, 1981).

Thus, if the athlete considers performance excellence to be an important value, then predictably, more time and effort will be devoted toward skill development, and the athlete will be fully engaged in training, practicing, and contest preparation. Failure will more likely be viewed as part of the skill-building process because the athlete's reaction to failure will be constructive. The athlete will consider performance success as a core value and be fully engaged in all areas of physical and mental contest preparation. A disconnect between the athlete's values and behavior patterns will be unlikely. A typical list of values that form the basis of the DVM is in the box below.

Values Checklist

___ Beauty	___ Kindness
___ Health	___ Knowledge
___ Concern for others	___ Loyalty
___ Humor	___ Perseverance
___ Character	___ Respect for others
___ Humility	___ Responsibility
___ Commitment	___ Security
___ Integrity	___ Serenity
___ Compassion	___ Service to others
___ Courage	___ Wealth
___ Creativity	___ Family
___ Excellence	___ Freedom
___ Faith	___ Generosity
___ Fairness	___ Genuineness
___ Happiness	

CONCLUDING COMMENTS

Including a chapter on *exercise failure* is based on numerous studies showing that people who begin a formal exercise program will not maintain it within 6 months of starting it. In fact, the dropout rate of most exercise programs is close to 50% of those who start a formal program. Exercise failure is likely to blame for this unfortunate tendency.

How do we motivate people to change their lifestyle, from inactive to active, and not return to a potentially fatal sedentary lifestyle? How can we instill a strong exercise ethic in our children that will endure over a lifetime, leading to more physical activity in adulthood? To prevent injury and pain, how do we replace a typical exercise regimen perceived as grueling, overly difficult, and unpleasant with a less intense, pleasant approach that is viewed by exercisers as enjoyable, even fun? Exercise, if performed correctly, need not be painful or even unpleasant. People need to overcome exercise failure and dropout, especially adults who are older, overweight, have joint problems, cannot afford fitness club memberships, and lead a sedentary lifestyle. We need to be sensitive to the limitations of exercise novices so that we slowly build rituals into their schedule—rituals that are consistent with their values (e.g., health, family, faith, happiness).

CONCLUSION

If you're not failing, you're not growing

—author H. Stanley Judd (Zoë B., 2013)

This section summarizes key points and takeaways and also points out the benefits of, and proper responses to, failing. What should readers know after reading this book that will improve performance, physical health, and mental well-being?

Readers need to be reminded that failure can—and should—result in productive and desirable outcomes. Failure should be a useful experience, but it is useless if performers do not learn from the experience. The likelihood of future failure is vastly reduced if a person creates the energy and effort to learn from experience. Eventually, we want to become immune to the unpleasant effects of failure and, instead, to turn failure into the constructive and helpful experience it can and should be.

Feeling comfortable with failure requires forgetting about traditional interpretations of failure. The road to success does *not* require making others fail and celebrating "victory" over the efforts and skills of others. Positive failure does not thrive on within-team competition. Competition among team members may inhibit group cohesion—feeling a sense of togetherness—among group members. In addition, within-team competition focuses the athlete's (worker's) psyche with a desire to win rather than to solve problems and improve performance. Yet another undesirable outcome of within-team competition is to inhibit the sharing of information that is vital to innovation. This idea of having an advantage over other team members is reminiscent of university programs in medicine and law in which only certain students are selected to participate in the degree program and internship. Because only a certain percentage of students are allowed to enter the program, it is not likely students will share information that will benefit others. Within sport-team rivalry has the same effect. Thus, failure-tolerant leaders encourage collaboration because they know that sharing information through collaboration will lead to a better product.

Failure is more likely in some situations and under some conditions than others. One situation that virtually guarantees failure is sport competition. Athletes compete against each other and against their previous performance level to win, to produce a superior outcome, to be perfect. Because perfection and constant victory are impossible to achieve, failure is inevitable. Psychology professor and researcher Dr. Robert Sternberg said that "the major factor whether people achieve expertise is not some fixed prior ability, but purposeful engagement" (Dweck, 2006, p. 5).

HOW FAILURE CAN BE USEFUL: FAILING "INTELLIGENTLY"

A primary theme of this book is that failing has many advantages. There is a list of five benefits of failure written by Duke University professor Dr. Sim Sitkin (1992):

1. *Keep your options open.* More attempts at successfully completing a task or meeting a goal often means a greater chance of failure. Improving the odds of success is directly related to the number of attempts (e.g., shots on goal, throwing a curve ball on a count of 3–1).
2. *Learn what does not work.* Success is often a reflection of numerous failures. Computers, electronic appliances, and even applying strategies in sport competition have come from earlier failed attempts. In sport settings, team and individual player strategies often reflect the

competitor's physical characteristics and skills. The 1959 Chicago White Sox baseball team included several players with considerable speed but relatively little home run power. Consequently, team strategy was based on these player skills and characteristics: They concentrated on hitting singles and doubles, and stealing bases, but relatively little emphasis was placed on hitting home runs.

3. *Create the conditions to attract resources and attention.* Sadly, sometimes a project or situation has to fall apart before it can be fixed—or people in power require it to be fixed. Sometimes teams and individual athletes are less driven to fix an existing problem and, instead, attempt to generate a new project. For example, it would be in the team's best interests if the head coach made sure that the team had high member satisfaction; that is, all players were relatively happy with the way things were going. Sometimes, however, the coach will wait until there is a team crisis or team members argue, creating high tension, before the problem is addressed and, hopefully, rectified. Creating the conditions to attract attention might mean having regular coach-athlete meetings (individual or group) to sort out concerns in private and confidentially.

4. *Make room for new leaders.* Leadership is a skill, of course. And people in leadership positions have strengths and weaknesses, just like everyone else. Leadership on sports teams should be nurtured and promoted. If a player or even all team members require information, incentive, better physical conditioning and fitness, or anything else that is currently lacking, team members should establish their leadership skills in bringing up these issues to the head coach. A team may have designated team captains and coaches, but any team member can serve a leadership role in meeting an unmet team need. When the need for additional (or improved) leadership is apparent, it is time to address that need as soon as possible.

5. *Develop intuition and skill.* This is where team members can help each other. Some players might have competed against a current opponent and have insights into the opponent's strengths and weaknesses. These experiences and perceptions need to be shared with teammates and coaches. What are the opponents' tendencies or particular players who perform certain skills particularly well? What

skills need to be developed by a competitor or team unit? Sometimes experiencing failure brings out this information.

What this book and the literature it represents tell us about failure is the following:

1. Failure is a perception. An event or an outcome is labeled *failure* only if the performer allows this label to be used.
2. Failure is inevitable. This is because humans are imperfect, and life is filled with risks that will result in subpar performance, otherwise known as failure.
3. Failure is useful. We can and must learn from failure and develop our skills in sport and other areas of physical performance in response to errors and other outcomes that fall below expectations and goals. We get better from failing.
4. All successful people, including athletes, have admitted to failing—extensively, repeatedly, but constructively. It's called *positive failure.*
5. Leaders in sport and other areas of movement performance must help athletes deal with failure constructively and not overreact to imperfect athlete performance. There is a condition called *neurotic perfectionism* in which the person, usually someone in a leadership position (e.g., coach, parent, supervisor), is never satisfied with his or her subordinate's performance quality. "It" can always be better. Leaders need to recognize the importance of giving credit to performance quality and to performance improvement, and not refer to subperfect performance as failure.
6. Failure should be motivating, particularly with respect to building intrinsic motivation (IM). IM reflects a person's incentive to engage in an activity because it is satisfying, even fun. Increasing IM consists of the following components: (1) provide the performer with positive information about performance correctness and desirable outcomes; (2) deliver information feedback that enhances feelings of (perceived) competence, that is, the performer views his or her own performance as desirable, improving, and/or highly skilled; and (3) allow the performer to select which sport, activity, and position in which they wish to participate, a process called self-determination.

7. Failure in exercise settings should be viewed as a positive step toward improving exercise technique and fitness, losing/managing weight, being more mentally alert, having an improved physical appearance, and having more energy.

In her book *Mindset*, professor and psychologist Dr. Carol Dweck (2006) suggests that how people respond to mistakes and failure is determined by their mind-set. Believing that our qualities are "carved in stone" is called the *fixed mind-set*, while believing that our basic qualities are what we cultivate through effort is referred to as our *growth mind-set*. A fixed mind-set creates an urgency to repeatedly prove ourselves worthy and valuable. The growth mind-set, far preferred for future growth and learning, "is based on the belief that your basic qualities are things you can cultivate through your efforts" (Dweck, 2006, p. 7). The growth mind-set reflects the belief that a person's true potential is unknown, and that it is impossible to foresee what can be accomplished given the proper training. Errors and mistakes are an integral part of learning, improving, and growing. As Dr. Dweck explains, "Exceptional people seem to have a special talent for converting life's setbacks into future successes" (p. 11). And this is the main reason we have two definitions of failure.

The *fixed mind-set* indicates a need to prove you are smart or "perfect," and to engage in harsh self-criticism when high standards are not achieved. Examples of the highly critical self-talk of the fixed mind-set include "We lost an event," "I lost my job/got fired," "I received a negative evaluation," "I was rejected." Failure, then, is about not meeting your potential and your goals. People with a fixed mind-set fear failure and, therefore, do not take risks in going to a higher level and advancing their skills. Competition becomes threatening and produces stress and anxiety. The fixed mind-set is opposite to what this book is about.

The *growth mind-set*, on the other hand, reflects failure as not growing and not reaching or obtaining what you value. This mind-set promotes learning from failure and appreciating and valuing feedback. The growth mind-set illustrates the purpose and focus of this book. Failure is an intrinsic component of growth, achievement, and success. Persons with a growth mind-set are receptive to coaching and adopt new strategies from what they observe, hear, or experience. Failure is perceived as an action (i.e.,

"I failed") in the growth mind-set, whereas failure become one's identity (i.e., "I am a failure") in the fixed mind-set. Children who drop out of youth sports conclude they do not have the ability to succeed—"I am a failure"— whereas child athletes who stay with their sports program continue to grow and improve; they can isolate failure to specific acts and develop skills to overcome those early failures.

Sports coaches and parents have an important role to play in generating feedback and motivational statements that help young athletes perceive their performance as improving, successful, and enjoyable, and to help them remain optimistic about future skill development. Adults who encourage a fixed mind-set among child athletes are teaching them to attribute blame to others and making excuses in response to failure. A growth mind-set, on the other hand, teaches child athletes to take responsibility for their performance and to work harder to learn, improve, and overcome the challenges of competitive sport, even when performing against opponents with superior skills. Failure may continue to be disappointing, but failure is not defined by disappointing performance; they are not "inferior athletes." Success is about working hard to achieve. As Dweck describes, for the growth mind-set athlete, "effort is what ignites that ability and turns it into accomplishment" (p. 41).

A growth mind-set is a concept that is also related to children, as depicted in the following newspaper article written by columnist Susan Steen (2015), who is addressing parents of school-aged children as the new academic year gets underway. The topic concerns not expecting perfection from our children's performance in school. There are strong implications for sport.

> For parents of young students, I would beg them to let it be OK for their child to not be perfect. Sure, some kids are just wired to seek perfection, but more often than not parents and teachers make failure a negative and success the only acceptable outcome.
>
> Marian Wright Edelman had a great perspective when she said, "Failure is just another way to learn how to do something right." In a study at Queensland University (Australia), they discovered that one of the biggest problems for students today is overparenting. Overparenting is characterized in the study as parents' misguided attempts to improve their child's current and future personal and academic success. For some reason, we parents believe that our actions can ensure success for our children, when in reality our actions merely prolong our children's experience of failure. (pp. 1D–2D)

Apparently the perception of imperfection—not meeting parental standards—leading to perceived failure begins in the home.

What this all means is that *failure* is just a word, like *age* is just a number. Its meaning is in the eyes of the beholder. Unfortunately, success in our culture reflects the end result, called "the bottom line" in the corporate world, and not by the many good things that occur during the process of achieving success. To use a baseball metaphor, "won-lost records are not very revealing" (Will, 1990, p. 86).

Less understood is that failure is often a blessing. Virtually all famous athletes, including most members of baseball's Hall of Fame, failed early in their careers before eventually becoming sports icons. All-star baseball hitters, who competed primarily in the 1960s, such as Willie Mays, Ernie Banks, Hank Aaron, Tony Gwynn, Mickey Mantle, Lou Brock, Frank Robinson, Duke Snider, and Stan Musial each struggled in their first weeks, month, and season of competition, all hitting under a very mediocre .250. In addition, most of baseball's top pitchers struggled to keep their earned run average below 3.00 in the early days of their major league career (Will, 1990). Each of these players, along with many others who aspired to play sports at the highest level, possessed the right set personal characteristics. These included patience, mental toughness, hardiness/resourcefulness, receptivity to coaching (not defensive, arrogant, or obstinate), confidence, being well-trained, and being prepared to play the game at 100% effort.

How important is patience to a professional athlete in terms of succeeding and avoiding ultimate failure? Patience is a virtue in elite sport that relies on meeting performance demands in fractions of seconds. According to Will (1990),

> The toughest thing to judge [in baseball] is velocity. Good hitters see the ball right out of your hand. They recognize a breaking ball or fastball immediately. That is why a changeup is effective. As soon as the batter recognizes a fastball he still has a second order of uncertainty: What kind of fastball? What is important in a change-up is the speed of your arm after the ball leaves your hand. That's what convinces the batter [about what type of pitch is coming—fastball or the slower change-up]. . . . That's what pitching is all about, the deception of speed. That is why good hitters like [Tony] Gwynn are prepared to take a few pitches to gauge velocity, even at the cost of finding themselves behind in the count. They have such confidence in their skills that they think the information they gain more than makes up for their reduced margin of error. (pp. 207–208)

My own experiences reveal another example of the benefits of failure. I played 3 years of high school baseball with aspirations to play at the college and professional levels. That was not to be; the college players were bigger, faster, better, and on an athletic scholarship (I was a "walk-on," and after a baseball career of one semester, I became a "walk-off"). The benefits of not making the college baseball team included putting far more time into my classes and increasing my academic performance. My grades were better, resulting in successfully applying for graduate school and obtaining masters and doctoral degrees. In turn, this experience allowed me to pursue a career as a professor in higher education. We need storms in our life to water and help the vegetation grow.

At the end of the day, failure is to be expected; it is woven into the fabric of humanity and provides a foundation from which to improve and excel. Writer and journalist George F. Will (1990), reflects on the inevitability of failure in sport:

> Careers in sports have different spans and paces, but they all have one thing in common. They end, going downhill. Every baseball player is deserted. The natural attrition of skills spares no one. So there is an inevitable poignancy inherent in the careers of even the best professional athletes. They compress the natural trajectory of human experience—striving, attaining, declining—into such a short span. Their hopes for fulfillment are hostage to their bodies, to attributes that are short-lived and subject to decay. The decay occurs in public, in front of large audiences. The decay is chronicled and monitored by millions of people who study the unsparing statistics that are the mathematics of baseball accomplishment. (p. 320)

Still, Will writes, "baseball is a remarkably cheerful business." One reason baseball—or for that matter, sport, in general—is so "cheerful" is that it is "actually a refreshing realm of diversity. The games are like snowflakes. They are perishable and no one is exactly like any other. But to see the diversities of snowflakes you must look closely and carefully" (p. 323).

Thus, errors will happen, at times resulting in failure and defeat. But, as Will concludes, "master enough little problems and you will have few big problems" (p. 324). And that is the reason we must continue to praise failure.

EPILOGUE

We live in a culture that is driven by expectations of success, the pursuit of victory, and finishing in first place. We are often reminded that no one remembers who came in second place, even the silver medal winners in past Olympic Games. In addition, we are impatient; we want to experience positive outcomes relatively soon rather than be patient and earn our victories with practice, coaching, learning, improvement, and skill mastery—one step at a time. We also like as much adulation, fanfare, and praise as possible. We thrive on recognition and approval.

Conversely, and sadly, errors and mistakes, instead of being viewed as desirable and part of learning, growth, and improvement, are frowned upon because they lead to undesirable performance outcomes called *failure*. We need failure. This book praises failure because trial and error is in the fabric of learning, developing, and succeeding in sport and in life. Every inventor created his or her new invention after experiencing repeated failure. Literature abounds revealing how our best athletes at first performed dismally early in their career.

Why is failure so undesirable for so many people, especially athletes? Why do we fear failure? Because failure is perceived by athletes and, especially, by their coaches (and, in some cases, by their parents), as a demonstration of incompetence and low skill. It's rarely viewed as a positive experience. As this book promotes, however, failure is not only desirable; it's *necessary* in order to grow, develop, learn, succeed, and achieve. Failure is a stepping-stone to bigger and better things to come, if we would just use failure as information feedback to improve our skills to reflect our competence. While errors and mistakes form relatively short-term experiences (e.g., during the sports contest), failure reflects the accumulation of errors and mistakes that usually results in undesirable performance outcomes. But what do we call the outcome when athletes learn from their mistakes and errors? Is it still called failure? Our performance has improved, after all. Perhaps so-called failure should be perceived as success if it leads to the development of skill and improved performance, regardless of the contest's outcome.

Why is failure so difficult for many of us to comprehend and appreciate? We are a competitive society, one that relishes victory. In competitive sport it's called *winning*. Competition consists of comparing current with past performance or comparing our current performance quality with that of another individual or group (team). Winning a competitive event brings us enormous satisfaction, partly because winning reflects success, which, in turn, demonstrates our competence. Feeling competent fosters task satisfaction and intrinsic motivation.

Competence is among the strongest sources of persistence at an activity. People who start exercise often quit within days or weeks if they do not see results quickly. We do not usually quit tasks, programs, events, or experiences when we perform with competence. The reason is that engaging in a task that makes us feel competent or skilled makes us feel good about ourselves; it builds self-esteem. In extreme cases, the tasks that bring high personal satisfaction can become addictive—literally (e.g., running/exercise dependence or addiction). Thus, behavior is often driven by feelings of success and competence.

There is another condition, actually a disposition, that drives our distaste for making mistakes and causes us to fear and disdain failure. The condition is called *perfectionism*, a trait that has both positive and negative features. *Positive perfectionism* includes setting high personal standards and having high, challenging, but reasonable expectations of others. However, most forms of perfectionism are undesirable and referred to in the literature as *negative or neurotic perfectionism*. Features of negative perfectionism include having excessively and unrealistically high self-expectations, high and unrealistic expectations of significant others (e.g., sports coaches, peers, teammates, parents, family members), the perception of others' excessively high expectations imposed on us, extreme concerns about making mistakes to the point of feeling high anxiety, excessive needs for organization, and doubts about one's action, which can result in failing to take reasonable risks. Negative (unhealthy) perfectionism may also result in reduced satisfaction in an activity, perhaps leading to burnout and, eventually, quitting. Researchers tell us that perfectionism is related to fear of failure, anxiety, depression, and workaholism (Antony & Swinson, 2009). Failure is a very unpleasant experience and yet is inevitable. Perfectionists do not cope well with failure.

The problem with expecting, anticipating, and striving for error-free sport performance is that it will lead to diminished enjoyment and gratification as a sports participant. There are many forms and sources of sport satisfaction, none of which will be experienced by athletes who possess negative forms of perfectionism and fear taking risks. Enjoyment as a competitive athlete or coach becomes an all-or-none enterprise; either "Everything/nothing went our way" or "We played very well/poorly." I have observed sports coaches who require their team to run laps around the field after completing a game in which they *won*. In addition, exercise is used as punishment—a common "sin" among sports leaders and PE teachers that teaches our athletes and students to hate exercise, an attitude that transfers into adulthood. From a performance perspective, the perfectionist athlete is often preoccupied with not making mistakes rather than taking occasional and reasonable risks. Finally, perfectionist sports competitors fail to recognize the benefits of learning and improving from mistakes. Instead of understanding the value of failure, negative perfectionist athletes fear failure and are more likely to drop out of sport due to the negative feelings that accrue from the perception of repeated failure in which athletes feel they lack the requisite skills to be successful.

The genesis of this book, as is the case with most book authors, is the need to tell my story, a story that reflects going from earning a very low high school grade point average to reaching Dean's List status throughout my undergraduate and graduate college career. I overcame a considerable amount of personal failure to eventually achieve success.

Perhaps the main takeaway from this book is that *failure is good, even necessary, in order to achieve and perform at the highest level.* But, first, athletes need to feel safe in overcoming our culture's fear of failure. They need to feel secure in taking risks and actually welcoming failure; they have to feel supported and accepted by their coach, parents, and others whose approval and recognition they desire and need. Reaching their ideal performance state consists of the combination of having reasonable yet challenging expectations, and making—and learning from—mistakes. The adult community—sports leaders and parents, in particular, have to step forward to make competitive sport the enjoyable and fulfilling experience it was always meant to be.

Failure is a perception. It needs to be experienced, appreciated, and applied. To use failure to our advantage we need to feel responsible for our performance outcomes—good and bad. Enough failures usually lead to a more objective outcome—defeat. Defeat is never positive because it infers an undesirable outcome. Failure and defeat may be related (cousins), but they are not twins. Ironically, experiencing and having the proper reactions to failure can help prevent defeat.

In the words of British philosopher and playwright George Bernard Shaw, "People are always blaming their circumstances for what they are. I don't believe in circumstances. The people who get on in this world are the people who get up and look for the circumstances they want, and if they can't find them, make them" (Cook, 1993, p. 439). Shaw also said, "A life spent making mistakes is not only more honorable but more useful than a life spent doing nothing" (Cook, 1993, p. 517).

REFERENCES

50 famously successful people who failed at first. (n.d.). Retrieved from www.Online-College.org/2010/02/16/.

A teacher resigns due to failure-free school grading system. (2010, August 8). Letter to the editor. *Daily News Journal* (Murfreesboro, Tennessee), p. B2.

About Don Drysdale. (n.d.) Retrieved from http://www.dondrysdale.com/about/quote.html.

Alderman, R. B. (1974). *Psychological behavior in sport*. Philadelphia, PA: W. B. Saunders.

Anshel, M. H. (1986, March–April). Bridging the gap through research and a major league baseball coach. *Coaching Review, 9*, 59-63.

Anshel, M. H. (1995). Examining the social loafing effect on elite female rowers. *Journal of Sport Behavior, 18*, 51-63.

Anshel, M. H. (2008). The Disconnected Values Model: Intervention strategies for health behavior change. *Journal of Clinical Sport Psychology, 2*, 357-380.

Anshel, M. H. (2012). *Sport psychology: From theory to practice* (5th ed.). San Francisco, CA: Benjamin-Cummings.

Anshel, M. H. (2013). A cognitive-behavioral approach for promoting exercise behavior: The Disconnected Values Model. *Journal of Sport Behavior, 36*, 107-129.

Anshel, M. H. (2014). *Applied health fitness psychology*. Champaign, IL: Human Kinetics.

Anshel, M. H., Brinthaupt, T. M., & Kang, M. (2010). The Disconnected Values Model improves mental well-being and fitness in an employee wellness program. *Behavioral Medicine, 36*, 113–122.

Anshel, M. H., Kang, M., & Brinthaupt, T. M. (2010). Promoting health behavior change with the Disconnected Values Model: An action study. *International Journal of Sport and Exercise Psychology, 8*, 413–433.

Anshel, M. H., Kang, M., & Meisner, M. (2010). Developing the approach-avoidance framework for identifying coping style in sport. *Scandinavian Journal of Psychology, 51*, 341–349.

Anshel, M. H., & Lidor, R. (2012). Talent detection programs in sport: The questionable use of psychological measures. *Journal of Sport Behavior, 35*, 239–266.

Anshel, M. H., Umscheid, D., & Brinthaupt, T. (2013). Effect of a combined coping skills and wellness program on perceived stress and physical energy among police emergency dispatchers: An exploratory study. *Journal of Police and Criminal Psychology, 28*, 1–14.

Antony, M. M., & Swinson, R. P. (2009). *When perfect isn't good enough* (2nd ed.). Oakland, CA: New Harbinger.

Atkinson, J. W. (1957). Motivational determinants of risk-taking behavior. *Psychological Review, 64*, 359–372.

Brady, E. (2015, August 23). Participation trophies don't warp kids' outlook. *The Tennessean*, p. 7C.

Carron, A. V., Hausenblas, H. A., & Eyrs, M. (2005). *Group dynamics in sport* (3rd ed.). Morgantown, WV: Fitness Information Technology.

Chase, C. (2015, August 17). "Robert Griffin III Thinks He's the Best Quarterback in the NFL." *USA Today*. Retrieved from http://ftw.usatoday.com/2015/08/robert-griffin-iii-washington-redskins-best-quarterback-in-the-nfl.

Chenoweth, D. H. (2007). *Worksite health promotion* (2nd ed.). Champaign, IL: Human Kinetics.

Cole, B. (2008). *The fear of failure: Nothing succeeds like failure: How to bounce back from defeat and reach your potential*. Retrieved from http://www.sportspsychologycoaching.com/articles/FearOfFailure.html.

Conroy, D. (2001). Progress in the development of a multidimensional measure of fear of failure: The performance failure appraisal inventory (PFAI). *Anxiety, Stress, and Coping: An International Journal, 14*, 431–452.

Cook, J. (1993). *The book of positive quotations*. Minneapolis, MN: Fairview Press.

Cratty, B. J. (1983). *Psychology in contemporary sport. Guidelines for coaches and athletes*. Englewood Cliffs, NJ: Prentice-Hall.

Crews, D. J., Lochbaum, M. R., & Karoly, P. (2001). Self-regulation: Concepts, methods, and strategies in sport and exercise (pp. 566–581). In R. N. Singer,

H. A. Hausenblas, and C. M. Janelle (Eds.), *Handbook of sport psychology* (2nd ed.). New York, NY: Wiley.

Day, D. V., & Silverman, S. B. (1989). Personality and job performance: Evidence of incremental validity. *Personnel Psychology, 42*, 25–36.

Deci, E. L. (1975). *Intrinsic motivation.* New York, NY: Plenum Press.

Dillon, K. (April 2011). I think of my failures as a gift. *Harvard Business Review, 89*(4), 86–89.

Dominick, K. L., & Morey, M. (2006). Adherence to physical activity. In H. B. Bosworth, E. Z. Oddone, & M. Weinberger (Eds.), *Patient treatment adherence: Concepts, interventions, and measurement* (pp. 49–94). Mahwah, NJ: Erlbaum.

Duda, J. L. (1992). Motivation in sport settings: A goal perspective approach. In G. C. Roberts (Ed.), *Motivation in sport and exercise* (pp. 57–91). Champaign, IL: Human Kinetics.

Duda, J. L., & Hall, H. (2001). Achievement goal theory in sport: Recent extensions and future directions. In R. N. Singer, H. A., Hausenblas, & C. M. Janelle (Eds.), *Handbook of sport psychology* (2nd ed., pp. 417–443). New York, NY: Wiley.

Dweck, C. S. (2006). *Mindset: The new psychology of success.* New York, NY: Ballantine.

Essar, E. (1968). *20,000 quips and quotes.* Garden City, NY: Doubleday.

Farson, R., & Keyes, R. (2002). *Whoever makes the most mistakes wins: The paradox of innovation.* New York, NY: Free Press.

Feltz, D. L. (1988). Self-confidence and sports performance. In K. B. Pandolf (Ed.), *Exercise and sport science reviews* (vol. 16, pp. 423–457). New York, NY: Macmillan.

Gardner, F., & Moore, Z. (2006). *Clinical sport psychology.* Champaign, IL: Human Kinetics.

Ginott, H. (1965). *Between parent and child.* New York, NY: Avon Books.

Ginott, H. (1969). *Between parent and teenager.* New York, NY: Avon Books.

Ginott, H. (1972). *Teacher and child: A book for parents and teachers.* New York, NY: Avon Books.

Goleman, D. (2011). *Leadership: The power of emotional intelligence.* Northampton, MA: Morethansound.

Hall, P. A., & Fong, G. T. (2003). The effects of a brief time perspective intervention for increasing physical activity among young adults. *Psychology and Health, 18*, 685–706.

Hardy, C. J. (1990). Social loafing: Motivational losses in collective performance. *International Journal of Sport Psychology, 21*, 305–327.

Hogan, H. W., & Mookherjee, H. N. (1981). Values and selected antecedents. *Journal of Social Psychology, 113*, 29–35.

Jones, E. E., & Berglas, S. (1978). Control of attributions about the self through self-handicapping strategies: The appeal of alcohol and the role of underachievement. *Personality and Social Psychology Bulletin, 4,* 200–206.

Jones, G., Hanton, S., & Swain, A. (1994). Intensity and interpretation of anxiety symptoms in elite and non-elite sports performers. *Personality & Individual Differences, 17,* 657–663.

Karau, S. J., & Williams, K. D. (1993). Social loafing: A meta-analytic review and theoretical integration. *Journal of Personality and Social Psychology, 65,* 681–706.

Leith, L. M. (1998). *Exercising your way to better mental health.* Morgantown, WV: Information Technology.

Lepper, M. R., Greene, D., & Nesbitt, R. E. (1973). Undermining children's intrinsic interest with extrinsic reward. *Journal of Personality and Social Psychology, 28,* 129–137.

Lesyk, J. (2004). *Quotation collection: The nine mental skills of successful athletes* (3rd ed.). Cleveland, OH: Ohio Center for Sport Psychology.

Lox, C. L., Ginis, K. A. M., & Petruzzello, S. J. (2014). *The psychology of exercise*: *Integrating theory and practice* (4th ed.). Scottsdale, AZ: Holcomb Hathaway.

Marlatt, G. A., & George, W. H. (1984). Relapse prevention: Introduction and overview of the model. *British Journal of Addiction, 79,* 261–273.

Maxwell, J. C. (2000). *Failing forward: Turning mistakes into stepping stones for success.* Nashville, TN: Thomas Nelson.

Murphy, S. (1999). *The cheers and the tears: A healthy alternative to the dark side of youth sports today.* San Francisco, CA: Jossey-Bass.

National Association for Sport and Physical Education (2009). *Physical activity used as punishment and/or behavior management* [Position statement]. An association of the American Alliance for Health, Physical Education, Recreation and Dance. Reston, VA: Author.

Nelson, A. (2015, March 26). Why the best leaders are defined by their failures [Web log post]. Retrieved from http://fortune.com/2015/03/26/alyse-nelson-dealing-with-rejection/.

Newell, K. M. (1974). Decision processes of baseball batters. *Journal of the Human Factors and Ergonomics Society, 5,* 520–527.

Ogilvie, B. C. (1968). The unconscious fear of success. *Quest, 10,* 35–39.

Papaioannou, A., & Kouli, O. (1999). The effect of task structure, perceived motivation climate, and goal orientations on students' task involvement and anxiety. *Journal of Applied Sport Psychology, 11,* 51–71.

Phelps, M., & Cazeneuve, B. (2012). *Beneath the surface.* New York, NY: Sports Publishing.

Ravizza, K. (2015). Increasing awareness for sport performance. In J. M. Williams & V. Krane (Eds.), *Applied sport psychology: Personal growth to peak performance* (7th ed., pp. 176–187). New York, NY: McGraw-Hill.

Rokeach, M. (1973). *The nature of human values*. New York, NY: Free Press.

Ryan, R. M., & Deci, E. L. (2007). Active human nature: Self-determination theory and the promotion and maintenance of sport, exercise, and health. In M. S. Hagger & N. L. D. Chatzisarantis (Eds.), *Intrinsic motivation and self-determination in exercise and sport* (pp. 1–19). Champaign, IL: Human Kinetics.

Schwartz, L. (n.d.). *Koufax's dominance was short but sweet*. Retrieved from http://espn.go.com/classic/biography/s/Koufax_Sandy.html.

Singer, R. N. (1980). *Motor learning and human performance*. New York, NY: Macmillan.

Sitkin, S. B. (1992). Learning through failure: The strategy of small losses. *Research in Organizational Behavior, 14*, 231–266.

Smiley, T. (2011). *Fail up: 20 lessons on building success from failure*. New York, NY: SmileyBooks.

Smith. R. E., Smoll, F. L., & Curtis, B. (1979). Coach effectiveness training: A cognitive-behavioral approach to enhancing relationship skills in youth sport coaches. *Journal of Sport Psychology, 1*, 59–75.

Smith, R. E., Smoll, F. L., & Hunt, E. (1977). A system for the behavioral assessment of athletic coaches. *Research Quarterly, 48*, 401–407.

Steen, S. (2015, August 23). Amazed by Grace: Success often born from failure. *Daily News Journal* (Murfreesboro, Tennessee), pp. 1D–2D.

Super, D.E. (1995). Values: Their nature, assessment, and practical use. In D. E. Super & B. Sverko (Eds.), *Life roles, values, and careers: International findings of the work importance study* (pp. 54-61). San Francisco, CA: Jossey-Bass.

Sportsline. (2015, August 18). *The Tennessean*, p. 6C.

Webster's new world dictionary. (1984). New York: Warner Books.

Weiner, B. (1974). *Achievement motivation and attribution theory*. Morristown, NJ: General Learning Press.

Will, G. F. (1990). *Men at work: The craft of baseball*. New York, NY: Macmillan.

Wrisberg, C. A. (2001). Levels of performances skill: From beginners to experts. *Handbook of sport psychology* (2nd ed., pp. 3–19). New York, NY: Wiley.

Zimmerman, B. J. (1986). Becoming a self-regulated learner: Which are the key subprocesses? *Contemporary Educational Psychology, 11*, 307–313.

Zoë B. (2013, March 4). *20 iconic quotes on failure that will inspire you to succeed*. Retrieved from www.MindBodyGreen.com/0-7915/20.

INDEX

ABOUT THE AUTHOR

Mark H. Anshel is professor emeritus at Middle Tennessee State University in Murfreesboro, Tennessee (USA). Dr. Anshel received a bachelor of science degree in education from Illinois State University, a master of arts degree from McGill University (Montreal), and a PhD from Florida State University in performance psychology. Dr. Anshel has 140 research articles published in scientific journals, and numerous books and book chapters in the areas of sport psychology, exercise psychology, and coping with stress. His books include *Applied Health Fitness Psychology* (2014), *Applied Exercise Psychology: A Practitioner's Guide to Improving Client Health and Fitness* (2006), and *Sport Psychology: From Theory to Practice* (5th ed., 2012). Dr. Anshel worked as a consultant for the Murfreesboro Police Department for six years in the areas of wellness and stress management. In more recent years of his career, Dr. Anshel has developed, validated (in several journal publications), and authored research articles and book chapters on the disconnected values model. The model posits that people are motivated to change their unhealthy habits when they identify an inconsistency, or "disconnect," between their unhealthy actions and their values (e.g., health, family, faith, integrity, happiness, among others). Behavior change is more likely when the long-term consequences of maintaining unhealthy habits—maintaining the disconnect—are acknowledged and viewed as unacceptable.

His work with skilled athletes, law enforcement, and highly successful corporate clients over the years indicates a clear need to reexamine our culture's tendency to recognize success without acknowledging, even celebrating, failure as an integral part of achievement and success. To winners, failure is a gift.